Of Wine in the Jars

Wedding Homilies

Willi Hoffsümmer

Translated from German
by
James McGrath

English text edited
by
Steven Heymans

A Liturgical Press Book

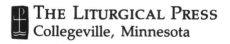
THE LITURGICAL PRESS
Collegeville, Minnesota

Cover design by Greg Becker

This book was published in German by Verlag Herder Gmbh & Co. under the title *Vom Wein in den Krügen* © 1990.

1	2	3	4	5	6	7	8

Library of Congress Cataloging-in-Publication Data

Hoffsümmer, Willi.
   [Vom Wein in den Krügen. English]
   Of wine in the jars : wedding homilies / Willi Hoffsümmer ; translated from German by James McGrath.
     p.   cm.
   ISBN 0-8146-2259-3
   1. Wedding sermons.   I. Title.
BV4278.H6413 1995
252'.1—dc20   95-20358
                                       CIP

Contents

Note from the Translator vii

Preface ix

Foreword xiii

WEDDING HOMILIES

1. The Sign of Love *(a rose)*   1

2. The Sign of the Cross *(a cross)*   5

3. The Pitfalls We Meet *(a butterfly)*   8

4. Concerning Loyalty and Preservation of
   Marriage *(a ring)* 11

5. Open the Doors to Your Hearts *(a key)* 14

6. The Fire That Must Not Be Put Out
   (a wedding candle) 17

7. Stay United *(a leaf)* 20

8. Be Living Stones *(a brick)* 23

9. Line of Direction Is Important *(a large spoon)* 25

10. Be Light for the World *(a candle with three wicks)* . . 28

11. Concerning Wine in Jars *(a jar)* 30

12. Supported by God *(a record player)* 32

13. Clothe Yourselves with Patience *(a small shell)* 35

14. Reconciliation on the Common Journey
    (a ceramic rainbow) 39

15. Concerning the Need for Friction
    (a smooth stone) 43

16. On Reconciliation *(a jump rope)* 46

17. The Rings of the Tree *(a cross-section of a tree)* 49

18. Marriage: Not Subject to Purchase *(seeds)* 51

19. Concerning Love: The Key to Heaven and
    Faithfulness *(a bouquet of flowers)* 54

20. On the Way Together *(a mountain climber's rope)* . . 56

21. Marital Companionship, Partnership, Security,
    and Much More *(bees)* 59

22. Concerning the Roots, the Trunk, and the
    Fruits of the "Marriage Tree" *(marriage tree)* 63

23. An Old Custom with New Meaning
    (bread and salt) 66

24. Help Is on the "Pilgrim Way" of Marriage
    (pilgrim shells) 69

25. Hinge Your Marriage on God *(a mobile)* 72

26. About Little Words *(a piece of fur)* 76

27. About Oil in the Marriage Vessel
    (an antique oil lamp) 79

28. About Farsightedness *(an embroidered picture)* 81

29. Seek and Protect That Which Is Precious
    (a shell) 84

30. About Dreams and the Good End
    (a kaleidoscope) 87

31. About a Firm Foothold *(a wagon wheel)* 90

32. About Fidelity *(a rosebush)* 93

33. Healing *(a small bundle of medicinal herbs)* 95

34. About Healing Water *(a holy water font)* 99

35. What Binds Together *(a large paper clip)* 102

36. Remain United with God *(a stalk of grain)* 105

37. Concerning Light in Darkness *(a decorated candle)*..108

38. On the Common Expedition *(a walking stick)* 111

39. The Sacred Number Seven *(a seven-branch
    candlestick)*.................................114

40. Latch on to Happiness *(a stepladder)*............117

Scripture Index 121

Note from the Translator

There is an Italian cliché that says "Un traduttore e un traditore" which is a play on words to indicate that a translator is a betrayer. In presenting this translation of Willi Hoffsümmer's book, it is my fond hope that the thought expressed in that statement is not verified here. It has been said that translation is not translation unless the music of a poem is given together with the words. Every attempt has been made to express the thoughts—not just the words—of the author. The thoughts expressed in this work are most profound while at the same time carrying a deep, spiritual message.

The ideas expressed in the homilies are unique. The author cannot be accused of giving platitudinous homilies, and deserves kudos for drawing lessons from such ordinary things as rainbows, clothes pins, a snail's house, etc., and especially for doing so while relating them to Scripture.

The talks are addressed to couples as they prepare to "yes" themselves into a life-long commitment. But the unparalleled images and thoughtful expressions found in the text are such treasures that they can be useful for talks on other occasions.

James McGrath

Preface

Marriage today is no longer the safe haven it once was; in fact, it is just the opposite. Now it is a "journey out to sea." The parties leave the safe harbor of life—their families, their neighborhood, their town or city, and, often enough, their circle of friends—and, as a consequence, they run the risk of an expedition, with all its uncertainties and imponderables. Besides fidelity and commitment, the word "marriage" in our day has taken on such new meanings as hazard and risk. A person who marries takes a dare.[1]

There are many young people today who understandably hope for the success in their marriage, but they also have anxiety about becoming shipwrecked. Both of these, confidence and concern, trust and doubt, are closely connected. Married life today has become demanding and challenging, and at the same time it has become humdrum and dubious as an institution. Many doubt their ability to see it through to the end. Yet there is in many the hope that they are capable of living with another person without conditions, hesitation, and doubt.

At various stops along the way of life, a person needs direction and signposts. One such important stop is the wedding itself, the point of origin for the common life of the couple.

[1] The author makes a play on the German words, *trauung, zutrauen, vertrauen,* and *sich trauen.* Generally they have a reference to *trust* but the word *trauen* can mean to put one's trust in, have confidence in, or to marry whereas *such trauen* means to dare or put trust in oneself.

At the time many are aware how much they are dependent on the help, support, and advice of others. But also at that time they are more in need of signposts. We Christians speak of the "sacrament of marriage" and, in doing so, mean that God, by reason of his unconditional love and loyalty, is with us on the common journey: "For where two or three are gathered in my name, I am there among them" (Matt 18:20). These are rich and encouraging words for marriage and family life.

"If we are going to get married, we ought to be married in the Church," agreed a recent group of college graduates. One girl said: "Promising in the context of the Church gives it more weight." An engaged couple from the course added that "by marrying in the Church we feel ourselves more closely bound together." The motives for the church ceremony are manifold and very clear. But behind many of the remarks just mentioned, lies the concern that we cannot do it alone, and that someone will be there to help and support. In Latin the words "to bless" are translated as *benedicere,* which means "to say well." If "the blessing of God" is to be on the marriage, then the married couple hopes that God is wishing good to them, that God will protect them on their way.

Highpoints in the lives of people are usually celebrated. Feasts and celebrations brighten our routine lives and allow us to put the humdrum aside. Time and again we must interrupt the normal course of our lives, take time out for thought and reflection, make our lives merry, and celebrate. There is an alliteration to be found in the German words *Festigkeit* and *Festlichkeit.* The former means "strength" and the latter "celebration." If young couples make the wedding day (*Hoch-zeit,* which literally means "high time") the first high point (*Höhepunkt-Höhe* is the noun form of *hoch*) of their life, then they will be strengthened (*festmachen),* and feel themselves more closely joined to each other. Their promise before God will indeed make their commitment weightier!

There is no celebration, no ceremonial rite, that has more meaningful signs and symbols and such expressive actions as the church wedding service. For that reason most people are deeply moved and affected when a young couple makes a lifelong promise of love and loyalty. Such an occasion warms the flesh and leaves no one cold or indifferent. Symbol and gestures lift up life situations of people; it is as though they reach out and give meaning and, in so doing, create a more meaningful relationship. Signs and symbols tell tales from life which give us bearing and direction. They build bridges between life and faith!

This book, with its many original ideas and stimulating thoughts, will help such bridge building.

Peter Neysters

Foreword

Doesn't it border almost on the ridiculous when, right after the wedding, the conversation is on to such superficial things as the style and fashions of the wedding or the food, while the church service goes almost unnoticed? That surely may be due in part to marriage homilies which end up trite and platitudinous. If the homily consists only of dry-as-dust references, rather than picturesque language, it is hardly likely that the souls of the listeners will be touched. But there are symbols, figures of speech, and stories that can be used. And if I give to the bridal couple something that they can visually "stumble upon" later in their home, then the thoughts of the sermon will be brought back in their conversations. (Lately I have been giving the couple a copy of my sermon rolled up with some kind of binding around it as a keepsake. If it is attached to the wedding book, then many guests can later call it to mind. Also, if the sermon is put on a computer, it can be done in very little time.)

Very often we work with couples for whom the preparation needed is minimal. Why, in such instances, dazzle with a sermon with the sparkle of a thousand-watt light bulb, when a candle would be enough? Sermons rich in symbols generate such a great echo because they take the couple away from the daily round of activities, from where they are, and carry them to that space from which we are called to proclaim the Christian message.

Perhaps you are concerned about the expenses for these ''reflections'' which often are great. However, in the echo which they release, it would not be an expense for us as long as there is a place in the parish budget for ''Sunday bulletins.'' Not only does it increase the attention of the congregation, but it also creates a ''feeling of belonging'' in the parish community if you enlist a hobby artist or a ceramic group to make a model of clay rainbows or snails.

And now you are making an attempt to preach with visual aids. Faith has to deal with risk! One need only make an effort, and the echo will inspire you to carry on.

Finally this comment: These collected sermons are in no special order; choose them as you see fit.

Willi Hoffsümmer

The Sign of Love

Preparation

Two roses for the bridal couple and one for the minister of
the service. Another option is one simply for the clergy person
who will present it to the couple after the marriage ceremony.
In addition, a card depicting a rose can also be offered which
will serve as a keepsake of their marriage.

Readings

1 Cor 13:4-8a, 13: *What love can accomplish.*
Matt 14:22-33: *Peter crosses over water (trust in God can carry us
over water).*
John 15:9-12: *Abide in my love.*

The Homily

I would like to present to you this symbol of love. It can tell
us something very definite about love:

1. We gaze at the marvel of this flower; it radiates beauty,
warmth, and tenderness. In the red of the flower's petals lie
summer, sunshine, and also passion. The scent it emits stimu-
lates within us the yearning for the one who has sent love into
our hearts.

But love, like the rose, also has needle-sharp thorns which
can pierce at any unexpected moment. But the power of love
is stronger than the prick of a thorn, and so usually gets me
through the pain, even if we have endured days, if not weeks,

of bitterness and coldness. The green of the leaves of the rose flower, which symbolize hope, remind me that a new beginning may be just around the corner.

2. I would like to share with you some reflections on the rose as a symbol of love.

There once was a poet in Paris who came upon a beggar. Instead of giving her the money for which she was asking, he gave her a half-bloomed rose. For a whole week he did not see her in her usual spot on the street from which she begged. But eventually she returned to her usual spot, only this time she was quiet and gazed in the distance. "What could she have lived on all those days?" someone asked the poet. "On the rose!" he replied.

He had gifted her heart, not just her hand. And it is precisely this distinction that this young couple must soon make: a beautiful home is important; vacations and a bank account can give much peace of mind; but, in terms of making a decision for love, these things are not everything! We must also give to the heart. We must make time for the other, to encourage and listen attentively. We must not let our love and giving become routine.

3. Another example of this is found in St-Exupéry's marvelous little book, *The Little Prince*. "Here is my secret," said a fox to the little prince, "it is very simple: people see good only with the heart. You can't be sure of that which you see with your eyes!" And a little later the fox said, "Throughout life you are responsible for whatever you have committed yourself to!" And the little prince repeated that and remarked: "I am responsible for my rose!"

(Name), you have made a solemn promise to your bride, *(name)*. Now you are for the rest of your life responsible for her. You are now responsible for your rose. And you, *(name of bride)*, have committed yourself to your future husband, *(name)*. You are also responsible for your rose.

4. Let us take another look at the rose. Even if the rose is withered after the coldest of winters, the five sepals still live. Could this be the reason the rose is the symbol of love? Love

in marriage should outlast even the harshest of winters, but this is possible when there is trust in one another, which can exist even if the feelings for each other have waned. You are here now to get help for difficulties; God wants to be with you, to keep you and to carry you through life, just as at this marriage ceremony the sign of the stole binding your hands signifies the Lord's help. When your strength lessens, remember the one who wishes to carry you through. Unfortunately, there are many married couples who have rejected the help Christ offers in their most difficult times.

That there are five sepals is not accidental: Five is the complete cycle of life; there are five kingdoms of living creatures[1] that represent the complete cycle of life, and also there are five of us here in the sanctuary, since the number five consists of two women and three men. These five are made up by the bride, bridesmaid, groom, best man, and minister. Apparently Jesus also knew about this number five at a wedding feast because, in his parable about attaining the kingdom of heaven, he spoke of the five wise and five foolish young women waiting for the bridegroom.

The number five comes up in other cultural contexts as well. For example, there are five points on a compass: the four customary ones—north, south, east, and west—and the fifth one which is the observer himself. To find myself, I am on an ongoing inner journey for which I must have a sense of direction. If I am going in the right direction, I should eventually encounter others and God.

5. A fifth and last thought is that in old cathedrals and basilicas, there can be found the so-called ''rose windows'' which face the west. The circular shape of this window symbolizes the shape of the world. Everything in it is pointing toward Christ who is at the center, usually with his mother, Mary, such as in the cathedral of Notre Dame in Paris.

As you start out on this common journey, it is my wish for you that your gaze be fixed upon Christ, whose healing

---

[1]*Monera, protoctista, fungi, animalia,* and *plantae.*

power and direction is very important for the success of your marriage.

Please take this rose in your hand as a remembrance of this hour. When it is dried out, please find a place in your home where it will be visible. In this way it will remind you of the thought I just shared.

Note: If the minister is holding a third rose in his hands, it is a beautiful gesture to give it to one of the grandparents at the end of the ceremony and say, "Without your love, today would not have been possible."

2

The Sign of the Cross

Preparation

A small cross of wood (or bronze).

Readings

1 Cor 1:18-31: *The message of the cross (in excerpts).*
1 John 4:7-12: *God sent his son in order that we might live through him.*
John 3:16-18: *Jesus came into the world to save it.*
John 15:1-5: *We remain bound to Christ (vine and the branches).*

Instruction

1. The talk has a special reference with ecumenical marriages.
2. Please choose one of the two stories.

The Homily

I would like to give you this little cross as a remembrance of this day. Please hang it up securely. And when you glance at it, call to mind one of the following thoughts:

    1. The beams of the cross demonstrate to us the essential directions of our faith. The longer of the beams says: ''Look back at everything certain; search out and love the one who ultimately holds the world in his hands. The love of God surrounds all that.'' The crossbeams say, ''Look to the side, es-

pecially at all the fellow humans in need. Love of neighbor is what binds it all together.''

Love of God and neighbor is the supreme command of Christ. You and your children must stand on these two legs—love of God and neighbor—if you want to stand strong and unshakable in the storms of life.

2. The cross is a sign of our pilgrimage. We are on our way to God, our goal and the origin of our lives. The horizontal part of the cross represents the line of the world from which no ascent is possible. The vertical part of the cross is the line to God who has pierced the hopelessness of the world through his Son. At the intersection of the world line and the God line is the Church, which makes access to God possible through the sacraments.

You have come to this church today by the power and guidance of Christ to take up the common journey. He came, not to judge the world, but to save it, as we heard read in the gospel. Elsewhere he says, ''Abide in me as I abide in you!'' (John 15:4). When I now wrap your hands together with this stole, the sign of Christ, this will become quite clear.

3. On the common way you can fall into guilt and sin. A psychiatrist can perhaps diagnose our compulsions, but only God can free us from guilt. The following short history makes this clear: A man wanted to get rid of his shadow, that is his guilt, but failed in all attempts, including rolling on the floor and drowning his shadow in alcohol. A wise man who heard this story commented that it was, in fact, not such a difficult task. ''How is that?'' asked a bystander. ''All he had to do was stand in the shadow of a tree,'' responded the wise man. For the Christian it can be stated: ''He had only to stand in the shadow of the cross!'' That is also the message of Jesus Christ to you as put by Paul in his letter to the Corinthians: ''The message of the cross is foolishness to those who are perishing, but to us who are being saved, it is the power of God!'' (1:18).

4. There is a story of several pilgrims, each of whom had become tired from carrying a cross. One of the sojourners

felt his cross to be too long. To solve this he cut off one end of the cross. After the long pilgrimage they all came to a deep hole. There was no bridge across the hole to the far land of eternal joy. So they put their heads, and their crosses, together to create a bridge across. The one, however, who had shortened his cross to lighten his load was unable to cross over.

The moral is that we must not avoid the suffering that we cannot change. In our passage through life we can also try to see how our burdens can help us. However I hope you may be spared from ever experiencing the full weight of a cross in your marriage.

Now, finally, may I ask you to make slowly and deliberately the Sign of the Cross which, for those of you who are not Catholic, I want to add, is really a universal Christian sign, and so you are invited to join us in making it.

With the fingertips we touch the forehead, the center of our spirit. Then we touch the center of the body, the center of the human person, and now we include the entire body in the Sign of the Cross and sign ourselves from shoulder to shoulder. At the conclusion we place both hands together; we do not form a fist, but make an open, sincere, joyful, and liberating movement. In this sign we have now been redeemed. May you keep and practice this sign as you journey together through life.

3

The Pitfalls We Meet

Preparation

A ceramic butterfly, or five paper butterflies.

Readings

1 Cor 13:4-8a, 13: *First there was faith, hope and love. But now love alone remains.*
John 15:9-12: *Live in my love that my joy may be yours.*

The Homily

I would like to present to you this ceramic butterfly (or these five paper butterflies, each representing one of the five kingdoms of living species) as a remembrance of this hour. Tape up these butterflies anywhere in your home—on the refrigerator, bathtub, on your bride, the wedding candle, or in your future children's bedroom. Some day your children will dance around you like butterflies, and you will tell them about this wonderful day.

1. Do you feel right now a little bit like a butterfly? After all, it is your wedding day, your day of joy, your day of celebration! Yet, when one is in love, it is easy to fly over fences, hedges, and pitfalls. We sincerely hope that you will live for a long time in the embrace of love and always feel like floating along like butterflies.

2. Experience teaches that sometimes we fall back into the caterpillar stage. When this happens, travel becomes difficult as we no longer fly, but crawl in the dust, bent over in pain and disappointment. But fortunately you are here before the altar where you can receive nectar, the food of butterflies. As with the caterpillar, nectar is also offered to us as Christians, first as a bit of honey put into our mouths as infants at baptism. Here, in church, honey and nectar come in the form of the word of God and the Eucharistic bread of life. Every Sunday you are invited to receive the nourishment you need to continue your journey.

Paul speaks in the first letter to the Corinthians about the supernatural virtues of faith, hope, and love, of which love is the greatest. Love brings you together. Faith and love can be lost, but hope—hope that a new beginning is possible—is indestructible. Faith, the first mentioned, is standing firm with God on both good and bad days; the faith we speak of is that which can move mountains.

Please join your hands and allow me to wrap this stole around them as a sign of your faith and trust. And remember that in Christ you have a companion who will guide you on your way.

3. The butterfly for centuries has been a symbol of the resurrection. Those of you who are unfamiliar with the stages of butterfly growth assume that the caterpillar has died when it pupates. But, as we know, when the sun shines on it, the caterpillar is miraculously transformed into a butterfly which can fly.

We believe that the Son of righteousness, Jesus Christ, by his resurrection and mercy, has rescued us from our caterpillar-like existence. When the right moment comes, when our membrane breaks, then everything comes out and life really begins for the first time.

With this in mind, dear friends, let your lives now be entirely different. Even if other people think that we are crazy because of our faith, our clear-sightedness will overcome everything, will turn human standards upside down and will release our unrealized powers.

You see, therefore, that these butterflies are not used just to remind you of your present feelings of joy, but they will also serve to remind you, in your low times, of the eternal salvation that awaits you. Therefore, they might serve as a guide for your marriage journey.

4

Concerning Loyalty and Preservation of Marriage

Preparation

The rings of the spouses are ready on the altar.

Readings

Gen 2:18-25: *The man is bound to his wife.*
Song of Solomon 8:6-7: *Set me as a seal on your heart.*
Matt 19:3-6: *What God has joined together man must not set apart.*
Luke 15:11-24: *The merciful father puts the ring on the finger of his lost son.*
John 15:9-12: *Abide in my love.*

Homily

(The priest takes one of the rings of the bridal couple)

When you see this ring from day to day, let it serve to remind you of the following thoughts:

1. *The ring is round;* it has no beginning and no end and therefore symbolizes your lasting loyalty to each other. In antiquity and during the Middle Ages a married couple would break their wedding ring in pieces if they were to be separated for a long time. Then, upon returning from war, imprisonment, or other lengthy separations, the couple would restore the ring to its original form as a sign of their fidelity until death.

The ring is a circular symbol of God. Hence, ultimately, only from God can you obtain the power and the confidence to remain true on good and bad days. We have indeed spoken of this in the premarital instruction: Loyalty means union only with one's partner in marriage—that is, no three-cornered relationship, and no conditions. You promised loyalty until death. At the prayer of blessings for the rings there are these words: "As the ring forms a circle entirely around the finger, so also the band of loyalty binds the two who wear this ring. We ask you, therefore, Lord Jesus Christ, to bless the rings and guard this marriage against anything that threatens it."

It is right to have sympathy and understanding for those marriages which break up; but please do not reproach the Church with anger for its prohibition of divorce. We see in the unity and indissolubility of marriage a picture of the relationship of the uninterrupted love of God for us. Jesus says: "What God has joined, man must not separate." The Church has kept to this word of God.

Unending loyalty means, therefore, that I am committed to you, not for a night or a summer, nor only when you are pleasant and likeable, but indefinitely. Loyalty for Christians means a commitment of lifelong fidelity, despite the ups and downs.

2. A life-preserver is also in the shape of a ring. If your trust in one another has become endangered by a third party, then I recommend you immediately seek outside assistance such as a marriage counsellor. No outsider can solve your problems, but they can help you identify the issues which are causing you difficulty. Please don't see such assistance as a sign of weakness, but as a sign of your strength and courage.

Likewise, please don't see your reliance upon God as a sign of weakness; indeed, it too is a sign of strength. If I place the stole around your enjoined hands, then you might see something similar to a life-preserver; you are now bound by the helping hands of Jesus Christ, if you do not forsake union with him. "Abide in my love! If you keep my commandments, you will abide in my love,'' says Jesus in John's Gospel (15:9f.).

In church we experience Christ in a uniquely intimate way. Participating in its sacramental life, especially in the Eucharist, is a way of reconciling ourselves to each other and God. In a way, the Eucharist is too a kind of life preserver which we should always keep on board.

3. There is a place in the New Testament where the ring symbolizes forgiveness in which an estranged son returns home to his forgiving father. While placing the ring on his son's finger, the father says ''You are no longer accepted as a slave but as a son (or daughter).'' This ring of forgiveness can save your marriage if, with it, we pass on to you God's mercy on whom we are dependent. We pray every day: ''Forgive us our trespasses, as we forgive those who trespass against us!'' One partner's willingness to forgive naturally discourages the other from abandoning the reconciling life that sustains us. You are thereby assured of the loyalty of the other party. ''The word 'forgive' is the best petty cash in the house,'' says a Chinese proverb. Daily forgiveness will keep you together!

Your wedding rings are made of expensive metal. The shininess of the precious metal can remind us of the glory of ''seventh heaven,'' which is promised to those who love. We wish you success, love and glory in your common life!

5

Open the Doors to Your Hearts

Preparation

An old key sprayed with bronze or gold, and/or two very small keys which can later be attached to the key rings of the parties without cluttering the key ring.

Readings

Eph 4:29-32; 5:1-2: *Good pieces of advice for a marrying couple.*
Col 3:12-15: *Put up with one another and forgive one another.*
Matt 7:24-27: *The wise person builds his life, his marriage, on rock.*

Instruction

Select from the various themes.

The Homily

I would like to present this key to you as a remembrance of this hour. It can be the key to paradise in your marriage if, that is, you take the time to look at it now and then. I have seven thoughts I would like to give you for the journey.

1. In connection to the word key, there is a beautiful love poem from middle high German, the author of which is not known:

> You are mine, I am yours: be sure of this.
> You are enclosed in my heart;
> The key is lost: you always have to stay inside.

I think the image of the beloved held captive in one's heart is a beautiful one. You shall forever be locked in my love.

2. In the readings we heard about a love that can open all doors. This universal key, "love," comes in many forms: respect, recognition, partnership, joy, forgiveness, peace, attention, and affection. Love is critical if there is to be security, trust, consolation, healing, liberation, and calmness. Only with the key of love can the last door of life be opened.

3. This key should make us stop for a moment and say "thank you" to all those parents, siblings, friends, and teachers who have opened us up to something. Momentarily bring to mind a "key happening" in your life. Now ask yourself for whom are you a key? Are you both now ready, as Christian people of God, to fulfill your obligations in marriage and family, in the Church and in the world? From the wedding day onward you are instruments in the hand of God, and by reason of your baptism you are called to open your hearts to others through friendship, hospitality, and cooperation. (At this point mention can be made of the associations, relationships, and organizations that have been part of the couple's lives.)

4. Jesus, in whose presence we have assembled, tells us: "I have the keys of death and of Hades" (Rev 1:18). Jesus, the "Key of David" (Rev 3:7), has opened heaven to us by the key of the cross. In marriage you bind yourselves in a unity with him[1] as your hands are wrapped here today with the stole. Your common life will be enhanced if you keep Jesus as your guide on the journey, for he himself has told us, "I am the way, the truth and the life" (John 14:6).

5. It might be that you, for whatever reason, have drifted away from Jesus Christ. If now you desire to come to know him more intimately I recommend that you consult the key to God and Jesus Christ in the book of books, the sacred scriptures, which play a central role in our worship services. In

[1]Him in German is *IHM* closely allied to the English monogram for Jesus *IHS*.

scripture you will find the words of life, the key which opens secret gates between one another.

Note: I always invite the couple to come to church services on one of the following Sundays so that they will get to know the parish in which they have just given their consent. On this occasion, I present the newlywed couple with a Bible in the name of the parish.

6. Prayer can serve as a ''charm key'' which can give guidance in the ups and downs in our life. By prayer I mean devotion to God and his son, Jesus Christ, through whom we abandon ourselves to God. Should a child of yours ever become deathly sick, you may feel a great power come forth from this ''charm key.'' (Also, do not forget the particular Christian communion from which you come; in it we are taught that you can pray together, for, when Christians are together in prayer and worship, there is no distinction among denominations. This ''charm key'' is also something you can give your children when they reach an age of understanding.

7. Perhaps you could hang the large key some place in your living room. I would also like to give each of you a tiny key on a key chain; but these smaller keys are easily lost. Notice how it cannot slip out of one's hand without the fingers feeling it slip. For this reason, it is not with the large key— the key symbolizing ownership, power, money or beauty— that your marriage can be saved in troubled times. With the money key every door can be opened, but not the door to the heart. It is for that reason you need this little key which has the power to open the gates to the heart through little acts like the gift of flowers, or a kind word such as ''I love you.'' Try not to allow these acts and words to become routine or empty by remembering the story of the rose and the beggar lady.

You see, dear spouses, I have prepared your common journey by providing you with keys. Perhaps among them is a key for the ''side door'' in your marriage, for that time when you no longer risk going through the big gate. We wish you that from the bottom of our hearts!

6

The Fire That Must Not Be Put Out

Preparation

A wedding candle (if the wedding party does not bring its own).

Readings

Song of Solomon 8:6-7: *The flames of love are glowing, powerful flames; even a strong flow of water cannot extinguish them.*

Matt 5:14-16: *You are the light of the world.*

The Homily

I would like to speak about your wedding candle because it is symbolic of a marriage relationship in many ways.

1. The marriage candle recalls your baptismal candle. At that time, when the candle was lit, Jesus took you by his hand as your guide on your journey. Today, he will once again accompany you and remind you to ''abide in my love . . ., so that my joy may be in you!'' (John 15:9-11). We see, then, that the wedding is a much longer celebration. As I put this stole around your hands, a stole that is decorated with the sign of Christ, this unity becomes more assured.

2. The marriage candle can remind you of your first holy communion which, undoubtedly, was a beautiful day in your

young life. But then came the stress and anxiety of adolescence which, for many, becomes a time of drifting away from the Church. But many return to the Church, unable to find any substitute for that which quiets the yearning of the human heart. Today, we recommit ourselves to Christ; be aware that Christ will be in your midst as you continue on your journey.

3. This marriage candle draws its light from the Easter candle. By his death and resurrection, Christ has replaced the darkness of life with light. From here on, you can always relight your candle when doubt, anxiety, or tragedy strikes. Now, as man and wife, you are to be a light to the world and Church. This is what happens when you answer *yes* to the question, "Are you both ready as Christian people to fulfill your obligations in marriage and family, in the Church and in the world?" Remember that "You are the light of the world!" (Matt 5:14).

4. The symbols in your wedding candle tell us much about the nature of marriage. The cross, which goes through the two rings, tells us much of the fidelity to which we aspire in marriage. From the cross comes a faith that can move mountains. The color green symbolizes hope in light of the many challenges that lay ahead of you. Remember that faith and love can diminish, but hope is everlasting.

5. You see your wedding candle gives light and warmth, but it is also consumed in the process of providing that energy. Whoever tries to outdo the other in service and humility, will become exhausted and burn themselves out, like the candle. So it is possible to overdo it. Instead, abide by the golden rule which says "In everything, do to others as you would have them do to you; for this is the law of the prophets!" (Matt 7:12).

6. Look into the flame of your wedding candle. There burns the fire of life which, just as we heard in the reading, is not to be put out by waters. The flame recalls the burning bush which burned but was not consumed, and at which time God gave out his name: "I am sent, me to you." You must always remember this name, both on good and bad days. Be-

ing aware of the nearness of God can comfort you as you go through life.

7. Seventh and lastly, the flame of this wedding candle reminds us of the tongues of fire of the Holy Spirit. We need you as spirit-filled Christians, not bored and humorless, but as man and wife who are "fire and flame." Then the city set on the hill will not be hidden (Matt 5:14), and your children will light their candles from your light which makes the world brighter.

Light this candle on your wedding anniversaries to recall this hour. May you bring light and warmth into your marriage. This is our wish for you!

7

Stay United

Preparation

A ceramic tree leaf (chestnut, maple, oak, etc.) or a freshly
fallen leaf.

Readings

Rom 12:9-18: *Fraternal charity.*
Col 3:12-15: *Love binds everything together.*
1 Pet 3:8-15a: *The challenge to harmony and to correct conduct.*
John 15:1-5, 9-12: *Abide in my love.*

The Homily

I would like to present this tiny piece of ceramic art to you
as a remembrance of this day. I suggest you hang it on a wall
in your home. When you see it, or if a visitor questions you
about it, you might reflect upon one of the following thoughts:

1. The representation is only a single leaf, but it is an
astonishing illustration of the miracle of nature. Each leaf is
different from all others, just as each human being in the con-
stellation of the countless millions of all humans is a distinct
creation. And, of course, each leaf serves a very important
biological role as oxygen producer; thus it not only keeps the
tree alive, but it contributes to the life of the whole planet.

2. The leaf needs the branch and the trunk in order to
survive. You too, lovely bridal couple, grew from the trunk
of your parents and grandparents. For that we must be grateful

to those who gave you the gift of life. Above all, we must give thanks to those who have instilled love in your hearts.

3. The branch and the trunk need the leaves to live. Likewise, children without contact with their parents are "deprived," just as a married couple without children is deprived. As symbols of the future, children become signs of hope and confidence as well as enrich the lives of those of us who are older.

4. One of the questions in the prenuptial questionnaire for Christian marriage asks, "Are you both ready as Christian people to fulfill your duties in marriage and family, in the Church and world?" The tree, which is dependent on the leaves for its survival, includes not just the nuclear family, but the entirety of relatives, all of society, and the Church. Just as creation needs leaves to create life-giving oxygen, so also society and church need families to keep them enlivened.

A crucifix was once found in a bombed-out church. On it was a Christ figure without hands or feet. The inscription on the cross read: "I no longer have any hands; you are now my hands with which you must reach out to the rest of humankind. I no longer have any feet; you must now be my feet." Or, put differently, we are leaves on the trunk of the Church, the still living Christ; we are the only Bible which will still be read in public. You, too, are invited, as fresh oxygen, to see to it that there is healthy atmosphere in the Church. We are dependent upon you. Dry leaves do not breathe any more.

5. Sap holds the tree and leaves, leaves and tree, together. In this sense, it works like love. Even in the readings we heard about the specifics of this love, how it shows mercy, kindness, humility, and patience. It forgives, endures, seeks peace, and is thankful (see Col 3:12-15). The parable of the vine and the branches told us where love comes from: "Those who abide in me and I in them bear much fruit because apart from me you can do nothing" (John 15:5). With this stole, the symbol of Christ, I will now wrap your hands together in this marriage ceremony. By this interlocking of hands you will be able, in good days and bad, to create new strength, much like a

leaf to the tree. It is our hope that you fulfill the wish of Jesus as expressed in his farewell sermon, ''abide in my love!'' (John 15:9).

8

Be Living Stones

Preparation

A brick, a corner of which has been cut off and gift wrapped.

Readings

1 Cor 13:4-8a: *Love keeps everything in place.*
Col 3:12-15: *Love binds the other virtues together.*
1 Pet 2:5-10: *Allow yourselves to become living stones for a spiritual edifice.*
John 15:1-5: *Abide in me as I abide in you.*

The Homily

In talking with couples preparing for marriage, I noticed that many intend to build a house. I would like to contribute to that project (presider slowly unpacks a stone and awaits the reaction of those present). Please set this stone out some place as a reminder of this day of your wedding. With this symbol in mind, I would like to share with you a few thoughts.

    1. If your house is to last a lifetime, you must be like a brick. The clumps of moist clay must first be formed into the shape of a brick, just as you were formed by the careful "kneading" of your parents, your schools, and now, your work environment. Then this stone was hardened through the fires of the kiln, just as you hopefully have been strengthened by the fires of sickness and difference of opinion.

2. Notice that at this spot I have cut off a tiny corner. In the process of drawing close to one another, you already have, or will soon discover, many blemishes or peculiarities in your partner, symbolized by the cut-off edge. The missing edge, however, can be restored. But is it critical if such a corner is missing? The answer of the master builder is "yes, it is critical," and that, with the mortar of love, it can be repaired. The mortar of love can smooth over everything and therefore remain an important building ingredient on your common journey. Even in the reading we heard what it can accomplish: "Above all, clothe yourselves with love, which binds everything together in perfect harmony." (Col 3:14 or 1 Cor 13:7). There is no limit to love's forebearance, trust, hope, or power to endure. Let us recall one statement from the New Testament, in which Jesus said: "The stone that the builders rejected has become the cornerstone" (Matt 21:42). Now let's add a third point to that.

3. The church is made up of living stones. Jesus is the cornerstone, and we as members of the Church are like the stones that the cornerstone supports. Now let me bind your hands together with this stole that is also a symbol of Christ. May you be stones built upon the cornerstone of Jesus throughout your marriage.

Take this stone with you as a memento of your wedding. May this stone of your marriage rest firmly upon the cornerstone of Jesus. Remember that "Those who abide in me and I in them bear much fruit, because apart from me you can do nothing" (John 15:5).

9

Line of Direction Is Important

Preparation

A large, wooden spoon or fork that might be used as a wall decoration.

Readings

Rom 13:8-10: *Love always makes you indebted to one another.*
Eph 4:29-32: *Love one another.*
Col 3:12-15: *Bear with one another and forgive one another.*
1 Thess 5:15-18: *Seek to do good to one another and to all.*
John 15:9-12: *Abide in my love.*

The Homily

I would like to present to you today this spoon as a keepsake as you begin your common journey. Hang it securely in your home. When your eye falls on it, you can ask yourself, ''Has our marriage become a journey to heaven or to hell?'' What I mean by this can be clarified by the following story:

There once was a man who wanted to see what heaven and hell were like. God granted his request, so the story goes. Having arrived in hell, he saw a large room, in the middle of which stood an enormous bowl filled with delicious looking foods. Around it sat people with enormous spoons, about three feet in length. All of them had an insatiable hunger for love, but each thought only of themselves, that is, wanted only to fill their own stomach; unfortunately, even with one's arm fully extended, it was impossible to get food in one's own mouth because of the length of the spoon. Thus they all sat in cold-stone silence; amidst abundance, they were still unable to eat.

In heaven the situation was the same: Again there was the insatiable hunger for love, and likewise the long spoons and the glorious foods. However in heaven a carefree, happy atmosphere prevailed. Here everyone was satisfied. Why so? They learned that with the large spoons one could only eat when each held it out to spoon feed the other! In extending their spoons to one another this was possible. Just think how much fun it would be if you would try that at your wedding banquet!

In other words, one's point of view is important! A slight change in the point of view can make the difference between heaven and hell—even in marriage.

If you are expecting to become happy in this marriage, there is still time to change your engagement. If you, however, decide to make your partner happy, then the marriage will be successful. Consider the following poem:

> If you wish to be happy in life,
> bring luck to other people.
> For the joy which we give,
> comes back to one's own heart.

Or:

> The way to one's own heart is through another person's.

In the "you" of the other person we can also meet God. I hope someday you will tell your children the story of St. Martin who, in a dream, saw that half of the cloak which he shared with a beggar was in fact worn by Christ himself: "Truly I tell you, just as you did it to one of the least of these who are members of my family, you did it to me" (Matt 25:40).

Sister Emmanuel lives among the garbage collectors in Cairo and Mother Teresa lives among the poor in Calcutta. They get power from the Eucharistic bread—Jesus in the bread—and then go out into the slums to serve Christ in the dying and abandoned people.

Now we are very close to the mystery in which you give each other the sacrament of marriage. I am only the representative of the Christian community, really only the ecclesiastical, official deputy. You encounter Christ himself in the other. And every time when you meet, love, and forgive one another, you renew the sacrament. It is as much a sacrament as when we go to Holy Communion or go to confession, in that we experience nearness to Christ there. We can scarcely grasp the magnitude of the sacrament of marriage. If we could do that, every meeting with the other would have to be an experience of Christ in that other. We pray that you will find this daily meeting with Christ in your marriage.

Now keep this secret before your minds: This stole, which is decorated with the image of Christ, is placed around your hands; you are standing here in union with Jesus Christ from whom you can obtain the power to have a good relationship with one another so long as you desire to remain united with him.

I would like to give you this spoon for your journey. Its purpose is to remind you of the other-centered nature of love.

10

Be Light for the World

Preparation

A candle with three wicks.

Readings

1 John 2:7-11: *The command of love to bring light into the darkness.*
Matt 5:14-16: *You are the light of the world.*

The Homily

As a remembrance of this wedding hour I would like to present you with this candle, which has three wicks, and upon which I will base my homily. Perhaps these wicks will inspire you during your wedding festivities to remember well this day as well as the message I will now give you.

First in importance is how much wax each one brings to the wedding candle so that the three wicks will have an adequate supply of fuel. Here I am not talking about your savings account nor your talents, but rather about your power to love. Surely, for this, one must express thanks to all who have planted this love in your hearts.

1. The first wick symbolizes the *yes* that we must say to ourself. You are bringing your entire self into this marriage, with all your gifts and talents. You are also ready to burn— that is, to give warmth, light, and direction in darkness. Your marriage has good prospects if you are thus willing to give of yourself. And those around you will receive some of the

light and love you have. You can certainly do that if you say *yes* to yourself, just as you are.

2. The second wick symbolizes the *yes* we say to the other. For the other partner must be just as ready to give oneself unconditionally. Anyone who wants to take it easy, whoever reserves the right to stay locked up, will never be able to experience real freedom in marriage. Such love with reservation puts limits on the other, while loving freely also frees the other to love in return.

Now if both of these wicks, which themselves say *yes* when the others are kindled, go out, the candle will of course burn crooked. It burns brightest and warmest when all three wicks are burning!

3. The third wick says *yes* to God. You have come here in the presence of God to light this third wick. Only in saying this *yes* toward God and the community of the Church, symbolized by your lighting the third wick, will your marriage begin also in the eyes and blessing of God.

From God a new hope, a new trust and a new love comes to you for your marriage, if you allow him to keep living in your midst. God holds you on good as well as bad days. This stole, decorated as it is with the sign of Christ, is a symbol of God's providence and protection. I will now place it around your hands.

As you begin your common journey, it is our wish that all three wicks will burn in equal measure so that you will make our world brighter and warmer and you will be able to watch over your children in safety in this same light. You heard earlier in the gospel that you are the light of the world. If there is no shining city on the hill, at least we know there will always be a brightly lighted window lighting up the street below!

11

Concerning Wine in Jars

Preparation

A beautiful ceramic jar or, as mentioned in the homily, two small jars as jars of life; between them a large "marriage jar." A small marriage jar may be given to the bridal couple as a memento.

Reading

John 2:1-11: *The wedding feast of Cana.*

The Homily

Jesus performed his first miracle at a wedding in which the water in the jars was changed into wine. Here you see jars in front of you:

Dear *(name)* and *(name),* the two little ones represent the jars of your life, whose content you, at some time in your marriage, will pour into the larger marriage jar, which symbolizes your unity in marriage. Later in life, your children will draw from the strong wine of love you put in the marriage jar over the years.

Do not put your prized possessions in this marriage jar, though. I have seen too often how quickly marriage jars are shattered as both parties look on. When I speak of the love which you are to put in the jar, I mean the ability to assess yourself, with all your gifts and deficiencies, so that you have a sense of self-worth when you enter the marriage.

Marriage is not an arrangement designed to make unhappy people happy. If you see marriage as something to do this, you are looking in the wrong direction. The wine in the marriage jar will not stay just because you desire it to stay. With time it will evaporate if you do not replenish it. Naturally there can be days when one of you must come again and drink from the common marriage jar because of some illness, trial, or crisis. Attention should be given if one of you is continually drinking from the jar, for marriage is a partnership involving giving and taking, taking and giving!

It is possible that at some time your wine supply will have turned to vinegar, will be very low in supply, or you may run out altogether. When you realize that you have no more wine, then you will have to do as the servants in the gospel: Fill your marriage jar to the brim with water—with tears, worries, surprises, and sorrow. And now you have good reason to say your *yes* before God, not so much because that is what the liturgy prescribes, but because Jesus Christ, who changed water into wine, will be the everlasting guest in your marriage. We know that Jesus was redeemed through his suffering. Today we remember that he also changes water into wine!

With Jesus, we pray that in the years ahead, the wine in your marriage jar will not become bitter or sour, but will become maturer, clearer, stronger, and finer.

As a memento of this hour I present to you this small marriage jar. I hope you fill it daily throughout your married lives. Eventually, when you drink from it together, think back on this day, and then think of the future. Occasionally you might put some fresh flowers in the jar.

I am going to roll up the homily you just heard and put it in the wedding jar so that at some more quiet time you may read it again.

12

Supported by God

Preparation

A small stand on which there is a record player and a single record which plays some song about love (from the instrumental part up to the aria). In many dioceses, the bishop has recorded a message for couples to be married which can be given as a gift.

Readings

1 John 4:16b-21: *Whoever abides in love, abides in God.*
Matt 22:35-40 (also Mark 12:28b-31 and Luke 10:25-27): *On the principal commandment.*
John 15:1-5: *Vine and branches.*
John 15:9-12: *Abide in my love.*

The Homily

I would like to give you the record as a remembrance of this hour. If some time later you listen to it on special occasions, think a little bit about what I am now going to say.

1. Most of the time a record has one side which you particularly like to hear which we will call side "A", the side with the hit. Let me say that your "A-side" is the side of love of neighbor. Marriage depends upon whether or not you have learned from childhood to be supportive of the other person. "This is my commandment, that you love one another as I have loved you," as it says in John's Gospel (15:12). Joy (not

only in marriage) begins at the split second in which we give up the search for our own happiness and try to give happiness to the other. The way to fulfilled love leads us to other human beings, even in our work-a-day world.

2. The "B-Side" of the record, which seldom becomes a hit song, is called "be yourself!" In Christ's principal commandment, which we have just heard, this message doesn't ring too loudly: "Love your neighbor *as yourself*!" This self-love is not to be confused with egoism, but is the foundation for all genuine love. First of all, I must say *yes* to myself, just as I am—to my appearance, to my positives and negatives. I do not love myself if I cannot properly love another person. And in that case I only cling to that person who then must drag me along. Because of the excessive demands made by one partner in a marriage, many marriage relationships simply die. Twenty years from the day of marriage, about a third of all marriages fail on this point. The reason: "I am tired of putting up with my spouse as well as the children who are only going to leave the house anyway. And while half of my life is still in front of me, I want to put an end to this."

The absence of a feeling of self-worth, in many marriages, is a cause of crises. If, for example, a person hasn't accepted one's singleness, he or she will never be able to live together as a twosome. As long as a person keeps saying *no* to one's situation, that person cannot wholeheartedly say *yes* to God. Self-love is a necessary condition for love of neighbor and love of God. Be truly the person you are, and not a poor imitation of some celebrity. Or, as it says in a poem:

> Say *yes* to yourself, just as you are.
> Only one who is merciful with himself
> Can be so to those beside him . . .
>
> Discover yourself and your worth.
> Only the person who respects his own gifts,
> honors the gifts in his neighbor . . .
>
> Forgive your own mistakes and brokenness.
> Only the one who recognizes his own limitations,

can forgive those near him.
God wills that you love him as he loves you. . . .[1]

But where is the love of God, which Jesus puts first in his commands, since both sides of the disc are depending on it? Love of God can be considered to be like this little stand here, which supports the record player, its fulcrum and pivot. This stand is easily overlooked, just as now so much is overlooked in our increasingly unchristian and irreligious world. If however this stand does not support the record player, then both sides—love of neighbor and love of self—will grind away.

The difficult word, *religion,* etymologically means to bind oneself to, to allow oneself to be captivated by, another. Being religious means that I trust in God from whose love I ultimately come and to which I must finally return.

For this reason, after your visit to the marriage license bureau, you have come here before the altar in order to join your love to the love of God. This love was already made evident in the engagement. Put your hands together so that I can wrap the stole around them so that your love is entwined with the love of God. "Abide in my love," we just heard in the gospel (John 15:9b); "I have said these things to you so that my joy may be in you, and that your joy may be complete" (John 15:11). So, preserved by the love of God, your love can succeed on good days and bad.

We wish upon you, not only the joy which you have received from this record, but also the joy which comes from your *yes* to your partner and to God so that your marriage may be a feast.

---

[1](Detlev Block, *In deinen Schutz genommen.* Spiritual songs published by Vandenhoech & Ruprecht, Göttingen, 1980).

13

Clothe Yourselves with Patience (Col 3:12)

Preparation

A beautiful snail shell or a photo of one.

Reading

Col 3:12-14 (-17): *Clothe yourselves with mercy, kindness, humility, mildness, and patience.*

The Homily

There are some married people who say: "The most important thing in marriage is to have patience with one another!"

1. For this reason I have brought for you this beautiful snail house as a memento. The snail is a patient creature. It doesn't run excitedly. It doesn't undertake too much. It is therefore not plagued by dissatisfaction. The snail's pace keeps it from becoming anxious.

Many married people today complain about the death of their feelings. Because of this, it becomes difficult to genuinely listen, to be emphatic and patient. Paul tells us in the reading: "Clothe yourselves in mercy, kindness and mildness. Bear with one another." To Paul's list I would add that we be patient with one another.

2. The snail can help us bring even more meaning out of the reading. Look carefully at its house. Isn't it a fine work

of art? How does it come about that no house is like the next! Do I see these splendors on my life's journey? Can I be surprised at the boundless inventiveness of God? How many other marvels God, in his creative throne, has prepared for us! We are of much more value than thousands of snail houses, or a flock of sparrows (see Matt 10:31)! Paul says you are God's "chosen ones" (Col 3:12). We must keep that before our mind's eye at all times. We are loved by God, are his precious creation, and are made in his image. The love which you have for each other comes ultimately from his love.

3. The snail shows feelings, so let me speak along that line. If I get too close to it, it creeps anxiously back into its house. I can provoke the feelings of my partner, make that person withdraw "like the snail." But this clearly disrespects the soul and dignity of the other.

The snail sees the world from below; the snail does not want to rule, but to serve. When Paul in the reading says "Clothe yourselves with humility," he is referring to conduct which can free. Humility really means "the courage to serve." If you pursue this conduct, there will be no need for either of you to crawl back into the snail house due to feelings of mistrust, caution, and anxiety.

4. Today we might say that the snail lives in a very unpretentious way in that it has everything that is necessary for life. Because of our limitations, we cannot leave good enough alone. We are continually making "improvements." The fact is, those who live unpretentiously acquire only that which they need. But acquiring possessions consumes precious time while not necessarily allowing us to live longer. Likewise, upon receiving a guest in our home, do we offer a drink and a bit of bread and then attend to them, or do we fret about, more concerned with food and drink but neglect the person at hand? "Martha, Martha," Jesus said, "you are worried and distracted by many things; there is need of only one thing!" (Luke 10:41f). It's not as if loving care for the comfort of the guests is superfluous, but we must remember that, in the end, genuine, loving care comes down to how present we are to

them. Young married couples also are in danger of being overwhelmed by such pressures as mortgages, finances, jobs, and lack of time that they can easily forget to attend to one another properly.

"With how little I manage!" is the message of this snail house. Place it as a memento of this hour on your mantelpiece as a reminder of what is essential.

5. On the snail house you can discover a wonderful spiral which either runs inside out or outside in. In the morning it can say "Live this day from your center out!" And when the daily routine overwhelms you, this snail will remind you to journey inward to find your center!

To find our center means to say *yes* to oneself, just as we are. Once done, I can seriously say *yes* to the other, just as they are. Having done this, I can also say *yes* to God who is our center and who is love itself. When Paul says: "Above all, clothe yourselves with love, which binds everything together in perfect harmony" (Col 3:14), he is bringing us to this crucial point in the sacrament of marriage: love binds all things together!

Right here at this wedding ceremony, this message becomes strikingly clear. Join your hands together as a sign of your love and I will bind them with this stole, a sign of Christ's love, which will preserve your love. Love is the tape which keeps all things together and perfect.

6. Often there is a snail on grave stones as a sign of the resurrection. The association of the two is explained by the fact that the snail in springtime breaks through its thick membranes before getting into its new life in its new shell. On a day like today we do not want to think about death, but if your love has to tolerate the winter of disappointment, mistrust, or misfortune, we take this occasion to wish for you, at those difficult times, a springtime of a more mature love. On this point Paul has a good observation: "Bear with one another and, if anyone has a complaint against another, forgive each other, just as the Lord has forgiven you, so you must also forgive" (Col 3:13).

So this snail house can remind you of many important things as you begin your common journey. I present this to you as a remembrance of this hour.

14

Reconciliation on the Common Journey

Preparation

A ceramic rainbow for the couple with the colors of, going from outward to inward, red, orange, yellow, green, blue, indigo, and lilac.

Readings

Gen 9:12-17: *The rainbow as the sign of the new union with God and a symbol of reconciliation.*

Eph 4:29-32: *Forgive one another, because God has forgiven you through Christ.*

Col 3:12-17: *As the Lord has forgiven you, so do you also forgive.*

Matt 18:21f: *On the duty of forgiveness.*

The Homily

In commemoration of this hour, I would like to present to you this beautiful ceramic rainbow. The rainbow is the sign of the reconciliation of God with humankind, as we have just heard read. It is simply the symbol of reconciliation. As Paul, in his letter to the Ephesians, reminds us, ". . . be kind to one another, tenderhearted, forgiving one another, as God in Christ has forgiven you" (4:32). Perhaps you could hang this rainbow over the door leading to your living room because it is there that many of your most intense conversations will take place.

The colors of the rainbow tell us even more about a happy marriage:

1. The most outstanding color is red. Red is the color of love. In his letter to the Colossians, Paul writes "Above all, clothe yourself with love, which binds everything together in perfect harmony" (Col 3:14). Now, as I place this stole, which is decorated with the sign of Jesus Christ, around your hands, love will flow into each of you; it is this mutual love and the love of God which embraces all; it is this love of God from which your love springs and flows back into both. Of this two-sided love, it is written in one of the books of the Old Testament, "Set me as a seal on your heart;/ as a seal upon your arm;/ for love is strong as death,/ passion fierce as the grave./ Its flashes are flashes of fire, a raging flame./ Many waters cannot quench love,/ neither can floods drown it./ If one offered for love all the wealth of his house, it would be utterly scorned" (Song of Solomon 8:6). And in a song of praise, Paul says that love "bears all things, believes all things, hopes all things, endures all things" (1 Cor 13:7). Love never ceases; it is greater even than faith and hope; it is sparks from the fire and fullness of God.

2. Then comes the color orange. With that I think of the sunset, vacation, and free time. If the marriage is to succeed, there must be times for relaxation for each of the parties. Quiet and rest sharpen our minds for patient listening and for the marvels on the journey. Those who are worried about money become anxious and stressed. Accordingly, they should not be surprised to find one day that their soul is dying and, as a result, that they have become deaf and blind to the heartbeats of others.

3. Next comes the color yellow. It symbolizes rays of the sun which, through cheerfulness, joy, and affection, evaporate the many clouds of sadness and pain which can move in. The sun is also the symbol for God. We desire that in your mar-

riage the sun will always follow you, bringing with it loving kindness and rapport. In any situation, you may worry about matters of church or state or your future children, but you may never doubt about the mercy of God.

4. The next color is green, the color of hope. It is the "little sister" among the three supernatural virtues, faith, hope, and charity. Faith can quell doubt; love can heal hate. Hope, which never perishes, creates a new beginning, provides alternatives at seemingly hopeless times. We wish for you this unconditional hope.

5. The color blue reminds us of the cloudless heavens. Couples often dream that their marriage will bring about a kind of heaven on earth, a "seventh heaven," in which we experience a few seconds in paradise—a comfortable home, the immersing into each other, and security.

6. Then comes the color indigo, a darker blue. This represents loyalty and trust. Loyalty means less today and, because it can be misused, it is increasingly experienced only with strings attached. Fidelity in good days and bad "until death do you part" may be humanly impossible. But what is lacking in power will be made up for by trust in God. Faith can sustain, walk over water and move mountains. It is for this reason that you stand here before the altar. With this trust in God's help on your common journey, you can go forth in good faith.

7. Finally, the color violet. We recognize it as the ecclesiastical color for Advent and Lent; it is also the color symbolizing the sacrament of penance. It reminds us of being able to wait, of patience and change, of forgiveness and reconciliation. With this we are closing the circle of the seven colors. The meaning of this takes us back to what I said at the beginning about the rainbow—it being the sign of reconciliation. "The word *forgiveness* is the best cash in the house," says an old Chinese proverb. Or, in the words of the Our Father which we so often pray: "Forgive us our trespasses as we forgive those who trespass against us." Since God forgives us time and again, our own forgiveness must never be withheld.

We know that a rainbow comes about through water encountering the sun. But if the sun of your love gets a dowse of cold water, you had better have your forgiveness ready. Under your rainbow of reconciliation you can always get together again. That is our wish for you every day of your shared life.

15

Concerning the Need for Friction

Preparation

A large, round stone taken from the bottom of a stream.

Readings

Eph 4:29-32; 5:1-2: *Good pieces of advice for a marrying couple.*
Col 3:12-15: *Bear with one another and forgive one another.*
Matt 7:24-27: *Build your life, your marriage, on a rock foundation.*

The Homily

As a remembrance of this hour I would like to present you something which I looked for during my vacation near a mountain stream, namely this round stone. You can threaten to throw it at anyone who tries to break up your marriage. Naturally, you can also place it in a flower box as a decoration or put it somewhere in your house. In any case, I want it to serve as a reminder of the following three thoughts:

1. When this stone broke off, high up in the mountain range, it was sharp-edged and capable of causing injury. By being exposed for millions of years to rain and running water, however, it has become smooth and refined. How often it might have "cried out" in pain as it was ground on other stones, when an edge was broken off and, as a result, it was little by little smoothed out. And now you see how it has been made smooth; as a result it can no longer be scratched or chipped.

This is an image for you. You, too, throughout life, are subjected to this process. Everyone has edges and chips. It can be painful to be in continuous company with one another to have the harmful edges filed off. And this filing will always be a part of your marriage. There are still many sharp corners. In that case no false compromises should be made, but only the readiness to face up to one another and to resolve conflicts. I give you a beautiful, round stone to serve as a reminder of this dynamic. Our conflicts for a while will be annoying. Eventually, however, we come to navigable water in which we cut one another less because our rough edges are worn off.

2. The appearance of this stone corresponds roughly to the many types of religions and people. Even the Chinese symbol of the Yin-Yang, which symbolizes the struggle between good and evil as found in Eastern religions, tells us something here; it is a symbol of the loving union in a metaphorical sense of the good, which is active, and the bad, which is passive—that is, it is symbolic of the harmony between heaven and earth which can be found only if held jointly. Both come together in their complementary relation of giving and taking, taking and giving. Yet this circle is not self-contained. The two can be drawn out of the circle, through the other, by the desire to be with that which is beyond. This "that which is beyond" we call God.

"Religion" means nothing more than "to bind oneself to the significant other." You will find that out. Even if the two of you were to achieve perfect harmony, you would still find something missing. Humans still long for something else to satisfy the soul. For those who do not have this spiritual longing, passion becomes a substitute. Passion is the opposite of longing. Regarding these passions I do not have much to say. You yourselves know how many misdirected yearnings there are which seduce us. This is something your children must be taught if they too are not to become entirely empty within.

I found a literary passage which deals with this longing for another: "Human beings who love must be grounded in the great love of the Merciful God." Here, I find the words "Merciful God, have mercy," interesting, as mercy and forgiveness are related. And the word "forgiveness," as the Chinese proverb says, is the best coin in the house. But Christian scriptures are even more forceful: "How many times must I forgive my brother?" asks Peter, to which the Lord responds, "Not seven times, but, I tell you, seventy times seven times" (Matt 18:22). This is to be employed especially when the other has become a "stumbling block." If you summon time and again the strength for forgiveness, which you can obtain from the limitless mercy of God, then we need have no concern about your common journey.

If the second thought appears too difficult to understand, use this alternative: Stand together, even if the other party is being stubborn. Remember that Jesus admonished his fellow Jews, "Let anyone among you who is without sin be the first to throw a stone at her" (John 8:7).

3. We heard in the gospel of a wise man who built his house on hard rock so that it might not be destroyed in the storms of life. If you build your wedded life on hard rock, that is, take to heart and make real the words of Jesus, then you will stand firm as a rock on good and bad days. How much Christ will protect you will now become crystal clear in the marriage ceremony. I will wrap this stole, the symbol of Christ, around your hands as you hold them together in order that your love will stand firm against the attacks of the evil one. As long as you allow him to be the first in your marriage union, you will be assured of his help and support in "sickness and in health."

May this stone serve to remind you of these reflections. And may the bright glimmer of this stone be like stars from the "seventh heaven," which we all wish for you on your common journey!

16

On Reconciliation

Preparation

A jump rope with a knot in it.

Readings

Eph 4:29-32; 5:1-2: *Good pieces of advice for married couples.*
Col 3:12-15: *Put up with one another and forgive one another.*
1 Pet 3:8-15a: *A call for harmony and for good attitudes.*
Matt 5:23-26: *Reconcile yourself first.*
Matt 18:21-22: *Forgive seventy times seven.*

The Homily

The word *forgiveness* is the best coin in the house, according to a Chinese proverb. Therefore I would like to give you this jump rope as a symbol of this wedding hour. Perhaps you can hang it up somewhere until your first child can jump with it, for then the toughest part of your marriage will be behind you. The toughest time in your marriage is not during the so-called "seven year itch," but occurs, as statistics show, in the fourth year of your marriage.

You see that this jump rope has a knot—symbolic of the problems which await you in your marriage. How is it possible that an argument, even a conflict between you, is resolved in a way that brings you closer together?

St. Nicholas of Flüe, patron saint of Switzerland, offered a solution when he held up such a rope to the quarreling Swiss citizens and asked, "How can I unfasten this knot? Will it happen if each pulls from his or her side? In that way it only gets tighter! And also if one side gives up, the other side only pulls further away. Then the knot remains and the problem is not resolved." There is only one way that the problem is resolved: both sides must give up their intransigence, put their heads together and, with united effort, just as in that proverb, pluck away at the knot.

1. As it was pointed out to us in the readings, a reconciliation is possible only if the words "pardon me!", "forgive me!", "come, let's make up again!" are not empty words. If you do not wish to destroy your spiritual relationship, then before nightfall speak a word of reconciliation.

2. A reconciliation is possible only if two continually growing partners are facing each other. By that I mean each of you must mature so that each can say *yes* to oneself, just as you are, with one's talents and with one's shortcomings. Inadequate self-understanding of one of the partners can be a cause for a marriage crisis. Marriage counselors show this clearly: Those who enter marriage with inordinate demands on the other partner only shackle themselves and the marriage. Anyone who can say *yes* to oneself, can say *yes* to their partner as they are, not as they should be. A person is ready for the reconciliation which frees only when they are capable of real compromise.

3. Nicholas of Flüe by those words is saying nothing new, and it is wonderful that he in that sermon was able to bring to a halt the conflict of his fellow citizens in the town war. Indeed whoever is challenged in one's own life can reread that passage and see that all his words and deeds were guided by prayer and fasting. And I would like to present those ideas to you. The most important things in our life must be suffered through and be directed by prayer. If you remember this, your togetherness and your ability to reconcile will be firmly rooted.

With this stole, which is a sign of Christ, I will bind your hands together. Remember that Christ is the first in your union; he is your creator and redeemer who will keep you in good and bad days, in sickness and in health. If you stay bound to him in your thoughts, conduct, and prayers, the success of your marriage is greatly increased. And I will be happy if I can see the day when your child is jumping with this rope, a rope without too many knots!

17

The Rings of the Tree

Preparation

The presider shows a real cross-section from the trunk of a tree. He gives two smaller, lacquered replicas to the jubilarians as a remembrance.

Readings

Cor 13:4-8, 13: *There remains faith, hope, and love!*
Matt 7:24-27: *Build your house on rock!*
John 15:9-12: *Abide in my love!*

Preliminary remarks

This homily is written for the celebration of a silver jubilee. It shows how easily even the other talks in this book can be reformulated for golden and silver anniversaries.

The Homily

(The homilist holds the cross-section of the tree firmly during the entire talk.) In front of us lies the history of this tree. The passing of each year is readable. There were very wet summers; these years are characterized by rings with greater distance between them. Many summers were so dry that the rings can scarcely be distinguished from one another. Experts can determine what kind of a year it was from each year's growth.

This cross-section of the tree trunk should recall for you the past twenty-five years of your marriage. *(At this point con-*

crete allusions should be made as to how the passage of time brought periods of much sunshine, as well as times of darkness.) Despite the mixture of good and bad days, your hope in the final success of things kept you together. Even more important was the role love played. Throughout all, your love endured. Just as, on the tree, the outer-ring must always be rebuilt with a new layer, so, with your love, must new layers be added.

On this cross-section there are some knotty places; at one spot there is even a crack which cuts deeply into the rings (which represent illness, misfortune, or fate). But it was always love which gave you strength and hope for better days.

I would like to point to still another aspect of your marriage as symbolized by this cross-section of tree. The more defined rings at the center provide the support and the backbone of the tree. They are not rigid, otherwise the tree would fall in a storm. These inner rings symbolize your faith in God. Religion means "to bind oneself to someone." Your Christian faith gave you stability in these twenty-five years. The sacrament of marriage should say "we have both bound ourselves to God," that the partner has been sent to me by God. Usually God gives for each task all the necessary graces. The more people accept this offer from God, the more likely their marriage will succeed.

In any case, all of us here today pray that, for the remaining portion of your marriage, you will place your tree ring close to God who is at the center. Then no stormy events will be able to lead you astray.

Faith, hope, and love are three gifts which constitute the fullness of God. With these divine powers may you be able to create many more "rings of the tree."

Please take these two small tree cross-sections as remembrances to be used for the remaining years of your marriage. I hope from time to time you recall today's homily. When you think back on today's homily, perhaps you can propose a toast to this happy time. Such memories of this time can help sustain you in the more difficult times.

18

Marriage: Not Subject to Purchase

Preparation

A little cellophane bag with flower seeds (perhaps sunflower seeds and seeds for little daisies) and corn seeds. The short story in the homily we had printed on thick, green paper with the parish heading. On the reverse side, on which the text is printed, the little bag of seeds can be pasted on the bottom third.

Readings

1 Cor 13:4-8a, 13: *The Canticle of love.*
Col 3:12-15: *Love holds all things together.*
1 John 4:16b-19: *Whoever abides in love, abides in God.*
Matt 5:14-16: *You are the light of the world.*
John 15:1-5: *Abide in me, then I will abide in you.*

The Homily

A recently engaged couple had a dream:

They entered a store. Behind the counter an angel was standing. Immediately they both asked him:

"What are you selling, sir?"

The angel gave them a friendly answer: "Anything that you want!"

The engaged couple responded without hesitation:

"In that case we would like luck and harmony for our marriage, health and success, strong faith in God, a readiness to work things out with each other, and to be good parents, if we are given the gift of children.''

The bride gave the groom a poke in the ribs: ''Oh yes: the end of all war in the world and in homes, the elimination of poverty, good education for children. . . .''

At that point the angel interrupted and said, ''Excuse me, dear engaged couple, you have misunderstood me. You can't buy any fruits here, we sell only seeds!''

With that in mind, at this beginning of your marriage I give you flower and corn seeds for sowing. Keep in mind that this is a symbol! Have joy when the seed springs forth both outside of and in you. For we all need growth in faith, hope, and love, so that joy will come at the common festival.

Allow me to reflect more intently on the bag of seeds. We see corn kernels, that is, seeds for livelihood as we need the bread essential for life. Since here on earth all nourishment is ultimately packed in a shopping bag, I might point to a broader meaning. The kernels must go through many changes before they get to the table as bread. First they must die in order to rise again into an ear of corn. Then it is crushed in the mill; and finally the flour is baked in the hot oven. The changes go even further. When we eat, it becomes flesh and blood in our body; and on the altar it is changed into the body of Christ.

This process of change of the bread lies right in front of you! Each day we die a little; in the scorching heat of life with all its stress, anxieties, and the twists of fate, we eventually grow and ripen into a new person. When we feel ourselves carried in the hand of God, these changes feel a great deal lighter. And so it is you are here today—allowing yourselves to be strengthened by the word and bread of Jesus Christ. Your *yes* to one another permits him to go along with you as your pilgrimage guide. As it says in the gospel, ''Abide in me, then I will abide in you.''

The bag also contains the seeds of the sunflower and daisy. We can learn from the sunflower. It drinks in the rays of the sun, which is a symbol of God. Whoever reaches out to the sun leaves a shadow of guilt behind them. And so we become light for this world (Matt 5:14). Or, as it says in the reading, "God is love, and those who abide in love abide in God, and God abides in them" (1 John 4:16b). Here I would like to express thanks for the daily sun that you have captured from your parents and friends so that now you can yourselves become like the sun.

The daisy offers to the world its small, fresh, quiet eyes. It is a very resilient plant as it blooms in the fall right up to the first snow; and in the spring the daisies stretch forth once again like thousands of stars from the dull green of the grass. We need people like daisies who, inconspicuously but happily, change the world in very small bits.

You are old enough that you no longer dream through the day. But take this little gift with you into marriage and go into the fields and sow it.

So what does the ending of this story mean? We all need growth in faith, hope, and love. With these gifts we will be able to remain in the common feast of marriage.

19

Concerning Love: The Key to Heaven and Faithfulness

Preparation

A red rose, a yellow and blue flower. Ideally a little rose bush, a primrose and a forget-me-not.

Readings

1 Cor 13:4-8a: *True love endures all things.*
Mark 10:6-9: *What God has joined together shall not be separated.*

The Homily

May I be permitted to present to you this bouquet consisting of a rose, a primrose, and a forget-me-not as a remembrance of having reached this wonderful hour. Perhaps you might dry them out and put them some place special in your home as a reminder of your wedding day.

1. The rose is a declaration without words of love. It should serve as a symbol of the fire of love. The passion of love is not to be extinguished. And it is our wish that, for you, that passion will burn throughout your lives! With the rose there also comes thorns. This, therefore, also means that I take you on good and bad days, in sickness and in health. So I beg of you to take one another entirely, with the blooms and thorns, with both the good and less than good qualities. With Exupéry I say to you: "You are responsible for your rose" for a lifetime.

2. The primrose in often referred to as the "key to

heaven.'' Since you are here, to close in on the ''seventh
heaven'' of love, I would like to tell you how these three keys
of a certain song (''Three Keys to Heaven'') open the doors
of heaven:

The song tells of a king who wanted to possess the keys
to heaven. ''When you find the right three keys to heaven,''
so said the angel who guarded the eternal garden, ''then the
primroses will blossom at your feet. With them you can then
open up heaven.'' For many years he was on the search. They
bloomed every time he saved something, which included a
flower, a weed, a sick wolf, and a wayward child whom he
took into his palace.

From that story it could be said that we must look for the
small miracles along the way such as the blossoming of plants
and flowers. Anyone who sees these precious works, also leaves
oneself open for the partner. Secondly, see in the animals your
brothers and sisters who are in danger. Anyone who takes
responsibility for the future of mother earth at the same time
carefully surrounds themselves with the treasures of the world.
And thirdly, don't enclose yourselves in a twosome, but have
an open door. Marriage involves hospitality to each other;
but the fruit of this hospitality to each other is hospitality to
those around you. The solidarity of the Church and the world
depends upon the solidarity of couples and the family. How
else can people genuinely stay together? With this in mind
you then pledge in marriage that you are ready, as a Christian married people, to do your duties in marriage and family as well as for the Church and the world. Thus the primrose
is the sign of the keys which will open heaven now and at the
end of life.

3. The forget-me-not, with its symbolic blue color, recalls
loyalty until death. Such loyalty is stronger than that which
can pull you apart. But the blue of loyalty is also symbolic
of faith. By faith I mean the trust that Jesus will give us renewed power in our marriage to be true in good and bad days.
Therefore rest your marriage upon the powers of faith and
loyalty.

20

On the Way Together

Preparation

A piece of a mountain climber's rope, about three meters in length.

Readings

Eccl 4:9-12: *Two are more on top of the world than one.*
1 Cor 13:4-8a: *Love endures all things.*
John 15:12, 13, 17: *There is no love greater than for a man to lay down his life for another.*

The Homily

In talking with you I have learned that both of you are guides for mountain climbers. It is for this reason that I am presenting you, as a remembrance of this hour, with a piece of a mountain climber's rope. Perhaps you might be able to place it where it can be seen in your home. And if someone asks about its meaning, or if you look over at this rope, you might bring back to mind the thoughts I am now going to share.

It is not outlandish for me to compare a mountain climb with your journey in marriage, for you are on the way together in climbing up the "mountain of life"—that is to say, climbing a mountain in which you also find God. And anyone who has already been on a trip up the mountains knows how inaccessible and yet friendly, how majestic and yet terrible, a mountain climb can be for us. Here we can really come face to face with the attributes of God. On the way to the peak we learn many things:

1. Two mountain climbers roped together are on a journey of fate. You can only reach your goal if you are ready for a partnership, in giving and taking, and in taking and giving. Perhaps one of you will have to give for a longer time if the other one is in crisis. At other times the reverse will happen as one tiptoes around the other. It is our prayerful hope that you will be unconditionally reliant upon each other. Today there are too many marriage partnerships falling apart on good days.

2. Trust in the other must also be present. If I, for example, am to be able to hang on this climbing rope, I must be able to leave myself in the hands of the other who gives me assurance. I would be weighed down with uncertainty if I were to think that the other party did not take everything seriously. Here I would like to point out to you the beautiful expression of the marriage ceremony in which you say "We trust one another; we trust one another on good days and on bad." Put your trust also in him who in this wedding ceremony now encircles your joined hands—the God, as the first in your union, who keeps you and holds you fast.

3. In the community of the two of you it is easier to overcome anxiety in hard times. Two see more; two boost up each other's spirits and carry a load better than one. A happy word and an outstretched hand permits souls to live through difficult times. The weakest one sets the pace. I must accept the other one as they are, and so accommodation and respect is demanded. What love can make possible we have already heard in the reading: "Love is patient; love is kind; love is not envious or boastful or arrogant or rude. It does not insist on its own way; it is not irritable or resentful . . . but rejoices in the truth. It bears all things, believes all things, hopes all things, endures all things" (1 Cor 13:4-8a).

4. Love makes it possible for both parties to deal with stress and undertake risks. You will never know whether in-

clement weather, falling rocks, or infirmity might threaten you. Hunger and thirst, cold and oppressive heat, are easier to put up with. Likewise, a comfortable home or a simple meal and drink will be that much more enjoyable when they are complemented with the affection of hearts.

Finally love is a gift that can be lost through inattention, habit, and needless finger pointing. How far does true love go for the other? In the gospel it states: "No one has greater love than this, to lay down one's life for one's friends" (John 15:13). Every year in the paper we read disturbing news about the fate of mountain climbers who give up their lives for others. We hope and pray that you will be spared this. But what these mountain guides show is what we wish for you on your common journey: In union with God and with Jesus Christ as your guide, keep words like *trust, community of life,* and *love* for the time when the going gets tough!

Before you pronounce your *yes* before God and this assembled community, I would like to share with you a mountain blessing which I read in the church at Neuhaus on the Schlier See:

> Protect, O Lord, through the intercession of St. Bernhard, whom you have chosen as the patron of these mountain climbers here in the Alps; protect *(name)* and *(name)* and grant them by your favor that, as they climb mountains and especially the mountains of life, they will succeed through Christ our Lord!

Marital Companionship, Partnership, Security, and Much More

Preparation

A ceramic jar shaped like a beehive (obtainable in stores) filled with honey, or a candle of bee's wax. Possibly, for the children present, tiny, filled honey jars, such as are found in hotels and in breakfast inns.

Readings

Eccl 4:9-12: *Two are better together than one alone.*
Phil 4:4-9: *Rejoice in the Lord at all times.*
Matt 6:25-33: *Learn from nature (the birds, the lilies, the grass. . . why not also from the bees?).*
Matt 7:12: *The golden rule.*
John 15:9-12: *Love one another.*

The Homily

"The basic necessities of human life," so says the Bible, "are water and fire and iron and salt/ and wheat flour and milk and honey,/ the blood of the grape and oil and clothing" (Sir 39:26). I want to tell you now something about the life of the bees.

There are so many miracles all around us! We live in a time in which we must open our eyes to nature if we want to survive. This candle of beeswax (or this honey jar shaped like a beehive) I would like you to put in a special place after your wedding. And when you look at it, may the following thoughts come once again to mind:

1. I will not talk about the busyness of bees because most of us work too much and live too little as it is. For the most part I think of the bee as a social insect. It is dedicated to community and cannot exist by itself. We humans are also dedicated to community. We need the security of a family in order to grow up as spiritually sound human beings. Certainly a living community of Christians is necessary for us to properly develop in our faith. It is for this reason that you will shortly pronounce your *yes* in the midst of that community which will support you along your way.

2. In a beehive, each bee has a job to do just as in a real partnership one must also be ready to give and to take, to take and to give. In today's society more change is expected of the man who has taken more responsibility for running the household. When I now tell you about the rotating tasks of a bee, perhaps you can take the lesson into your mutual living.

The bee at work in the beehive fulfills a variety of functions: it raises or lowers temperature by flapping its wings; it protects the entrance of the beehive, the "door of the house," against enemies; it looks after and feeds the progeny; it fetches the honey for life and winter. Up to seventy thousand bees function in that way in one beehive!

3. When a bee discovers a blossoming field of flowers—a so-called "munching site"—it does not claim it for itself, but shares it immediately with the other bees by dancing around it or by "a tail dance" which signals the other bees to come. If you can do the same with one another, sharing your joys and your experiences, if you give time for communication with each other and do not break off dialogue, then we will say of you what observers said of early Christians: "See how they love one another!"

4. A bee takes for itself from poisonous plants the good part—the nectar—and turns it into honey. You too must

choose from among the enticing and the hazardous offerings of your day. Because a bee avoids everything unclean, it is the symbol of purity. Test everything, but keep only that which helps you interiorly!

5. How much work making honey requires! For about a pound of honey a bee must fly around the earth almost three times! You too must work hard to build your "beehive," that is, to establish your household. It would indeed be nice if you left your door open. Because the bees leave their door open— that is, because they are hospitable—the bee keeper can carry away from the bees many pounds of honey. My wish is that you be hospitable like the bees. Thus you are being asked, "Are you ready as Christian people to carry out your obligations in marriage and in the family, in the Church and in the world?" Later when children come, you will notice how wide the door is thrown open!

6. In earlier times at baptism a bit of honey was put in the mouths of infants. This symbolized that we live from the honey of the word and from the bread of God (the manna in the desert was as sweet as honey; see Exodus 16:31). Therefore we gather on Sundays as a community of Christians who participate by hearing the word of God, which brings us power in the form of bread from heaven to actualize our belonging. (In the parish to which I belong, the doors are fashioned like beehives and, directly above the windows, bees are shown flying; this portrayal tells us to come in and strengthen ourselves with this honey! And after divine services, upon leaving, it tells us to go out and live with this power!)

7. The aroma of a beeswax candle can fill an entire room. And this tiny light is enough for me to become oriented in the darkness. So, in your marriage, you too can light up your surroundings, give light and warmth, and allow yourselves to be consumed like a candle. (Perhaps on the day of your marriage anniversary you might let this candle burn for a time as a remembrance.)

8. The beehive, the house of the bees, gives security and protection. Besides your families and friends, the church can

be the house to which you can feel drawn and protected on good and bad days.

So I wish you a very successful, happy, and blessed life together as symbolized by the bees.

22

Concerning the Roots, the Trunk, and the Fruits of the "Marriage Tree"

Preparation

A very tiny young tree, such that the offshoot is the kind found in the forest.

Readings

Song of Solomon 8:6-7: *Streams cannot carry away love.*
Rom 13:8-10: *Love is something you owe to each other all the time.*
John 15:1-5: *Vine and branches (abide in me, then I will abide in you).*

The Homily

I would like to present to you today this sapling for planting in your garden. It will be your marriage tree. Hopefully some day you will be able to relax in its shade and think back on this hour.

In this sapling there are roots and a trunk. If these remain sound and intact, chances are it will bear fruit.

1. The roots of this marriage tree have already had an affinity with your parents, relatives, and friends. The roots more or less say, "I can say *yes* to myself just as I am; I can trust in my partner and God; I am ready to allow myself to change; I can live simply; I can be affectionate, sympathetic,

protective, and supportive; I am eager for reconciliation; I can speak with my partner about little things and about my feelings; I am patient; I am responsible; I can still dream; and I can give and take and take and give. That, indeed, amounts to a lot of roots.

2. The trunk of the marriage tree represents fidelity, security, faith, hope, love, and partnership. The trunk is like a building site: Under the bark there is a very thin layer, the cambium,[1] a layer of tissue that remains throughout the life of the plant that allows for secondary growth. In it lie the living cells which build another ring each year.

Today you are here to contribute to the strength of this trunk. Your loyalty (which comes from the root word *drewo* which means tree or, for our purposes, to have confidence as strong as a tree!), love, and hope will be bedded in the loyalty of God. You will be able to see this clearly when your joined hands are wrapped by the hands of God as symbolized by this stole. Here is a cross of Christ, which will accompany you as your travel guide and, if necessary, will help you carry your own cross. It is so stated in the scriptures: "Abide in me as I abide in you. . . . Those who abide in me and I in them bear much fruit. . ." (John 15:4-5).

You might be entering into marriage for self-fulfillment—a buzz word in our time. But after the *yes* you express here today, please look for your self-fulfillment in the direction of one another so that the trunk does not break apart in a storm.

3. If the roots remain sound and the trunk is not stricken with lacerations, decay and vermin, the tree will generate much fruit—the fruits of satisfaction, good luck, loyalty until death, children and grandchildren, security, and cooperation in the community of life, all of which we wish for you in your marriage.

Please take good care of your sapling. Please stand here hand in hand in front of us. Sort out any caterpillars of in-

---

[1]Cambium: a thin formative layer between the xylem and phloem of most vascular plants that gives rise to new cells and is responsible for secondary growth.

difference and bring to the tree the water of sincerity. How green it can become if you do not hack away too many roots.

After Communion the bridal couple can in turn say this following prayer:

Lord, our God!
We would like to be like a tree,
which is firmly rooted in your earth,
with its branches outstretched toward your sun,
which does not break up from the frost of
lonesomeness,
but even in the snowstorm of hopelessness,
and after a wintery solidification,
once again experiences a spring.

O Lord, grant that no storm will split us apart,
no flash of lightning will strike us
and the material bark-beetles
which are lodged in the hidden crevices,
will not eat away at body and soul.

We would like to offer friend and foe shade,
blossoms and fruits to carry
and so give out love more broadly
which we experience more widely as gifted
to each other.

23

An Old Custom with New Meaning

Preparation

A sweet roll (pay attention to hygiene: put it on a paper plate and cover it with plastic) and a filled saltshaker.

Readings

Col 3:12-15: *Bear with one another.*
1 Thess 5:15-18: *How we deal with each other correctly.*
1 Pet 3:8-15a: *The call to harmony and good conduct.*
Matt 5:13: *You are the salt of the earth.*

The Homily

Here is an old custom. When the bridal couple cross over the threshold of their new home, they are presented with bread and salt. Formerly the salt was a symbol of stability and incorruptibility. It was for this reason at that time that marriage celebrations, friendships and treaties were sealed by the mutual eating of bread and salt. To this day, Arabs treat an oath taken with salt as something sacred. This bread and salt, which I present to you today, are to seal your sacred union. At the same time I would like to describe another possible meaning of this bread and salt.

The bread here is sweet. Today is your high point *(hohe Zeit)*, your exalted time *(Hoch-Zeit)*, and your wedding day *(Hochzeit)*. Hence everything tastes good. Perhaps at your next meal today you can eat this sweet roll as you share it together.

But let us think about the bread more carefully:

The bread has gone through a major process before taking on its present form. First of all the wheat must die, that is, be changed to rise anew in the kernel. Then the kernels are ground in the mill to flour. The heat of the oven changes the meal to bread. And when you eat it, it is changed into the flesh and blood of your body. This changing can go on even further: In the words of consecration at holy mass, the Body of Christ comes from the bread.

In many ways, a healthy marriage is much like the process wheat goes through to become bread. You will also be scorched in the oven of time—by stress, harassment, tests, streaks of bad luck, and of course the final change in death which awaits each one of us.

These thoughts should not stimulate sadness but give rise to some reflection. All these changes become easier if we put our trust in almighty God.

You can take this saltshaker with you into your marriage while you keep in mind the following thoughts:

1. Salt can cause ice to melt. If you look around you, see that there is so much deadly coldness between married couples, between parents and children, and among peoples in general. But you can be "salt of the earth," dissolving, freeing, and forgiving, just as it was said in the reading: "Bear with one another; forgive whatever grievances you have against one another."

2. Salt protects against decay. Fish are placed in salt so as to protect them from decay and rotting, which is caused by the foul places in the world and Church! In the gospel Jesus reminded us that "You are the salt of the earth!" (Matt 5:13). Keep the energizing force of the gospel, the message of God, unadulterated in your hearts, otherwise the decay of sin and error will eat away at you. See to it that you keep with you the words "Unity in marriage, indissolubility, and loyalty."

3. Salt gives a good taste. What would eating be like today—I think, for example, of soup or fried potatoes— without salt? So a marriage between two young people should

be a new flavoring for our country and Church. You are building the smallest cell. The vast body of the country or the Church becomes bland and burned out if the small cells are no longer fresh and sound. Give our societies new taste, little snippets of joy by your readiness to help and optimism.

4. Salt sustains. Perhaps you traveled once on a vacation to the Dead Sea. One can remain extremely buoyant without effort because of the high salt content. Jesus means the same thing when he spoke of the salt of the earth: It holds up those who are drowning, as well as those who need time to attend to their unfinished personal business—that is, those who are not ready to undertake marriage. Promise now to work for the tiny cell of the family as I ask you, ''Are you both ready, as a Christian marrying couple, to fulfill your obligations both for the Church and the world?''

5. And salt supports life! You surely know that on extremely hot days, the body requires more salt. Formerly, at the baptism of an infant, a bit of salt was placed on the tongue at which time the priest said ''Receive the salt of wisdom. . . .'' which means that we must give your life seasoning through the wisdom which comes from God!

Now you understand better what bread and salt signify in crossing over the threshold of the house. Since you are now about to take the decisive step, receive here this symbol which asks that we be open to changes; strengthen us with the bread of life; melt the ice around our hearts, and give our togetherness new seasoning.

Thus we end the marriage ceremony with the symbol of salt to remind ourselves of the primacy of loyalty.

24

Help Is on the "Pilgrim Way" of Marriage

Preparation

Two large, beautiful pilgrim shells (like those of the advertising signs of the Shell company). Perhaps for everyone present a small shell like the thousands found on the sand at the shore.

Readings

Gen 12:1-7: *Abraham as pilgrim who opens himself to the command of God.*

Luke 24:13-32: *Jesus, unrecognized, goes with his disciples to Emmaus.*

The Homily

Today, by your mutual *yes* made before God and this community of Christians, you begin your way as a married couple. And since our goal lies in another world, I must call your common journey the "pilgrim way." Perhaps you have traveled to Kevelaer or Trier. In that case you know that it is a very beautiful, winding, and strenuous journey.

For your journey as a married couple I am giving you this pilgrim shell; for centuries it has been the symbol of pilgrims and thus became a universal instrument which was used for many things, for example, as a water ladle, a dish, a spoon or a saw knife. (Perhaps on your wedding anniversary you might have an appetizer or a dessert using this shell as a dish as a remembrance of this day.)

Recently an old pilgrim path known as Jacob's Way has been rediscovered in Spain. "On to Santiago," as it was known in the Middle Ages, was used again as recently as August, 1989, when our Holy Father spoke at the burial spot of St. James in the presence of some 500,000 youths who were holding a Jacob's shell in their hands.

I have three thoughts to give you regarding this symbol:

1. Look at the shell in your hand. Each shell is unique and inimitable—just as the two of you!

I compare the empty shell with us humans in that, before God, we always stand with open hands. In doing so, we hope to receive his mercy. And because he says over and over his *yes* to us, we can in response to this compassion give to the partner when he or she stands before us with empty hands. As we say in the Our Father, "forgive us our trespasses as we forgive those who trespass against us." This readiness for forgiveness and reconciliation is crucial if your common journey is to succeed.

2. Pilgrims on their way to the grave of St. James pledged to carry a stone over their hearts. At the place of the Cruz de Ferro they were allowed to throw it away. As a result over the course of the centuries there developed a huge stone pile. Regarding that point, let me say that you also are carrying something over your heart which depresses you. Your and our final concern will be whether or not our faith and our deeds can stand before God. Will he be able to find in our lives the love he once gave us? It is my prayer that this concern stays with us.

3. You will run across a pilgrim shell repeatedly in life, most often at service stations where the advertising will say: "Come, fill up your tank so that you reach the end of your trip!"

This thought, that you arrive safely to your destination, has existed for centuries, for, in many churches, the holy water fountain was in the form of a shell. Also in South Germany and Austria shells are often found on the tabernacle. The significance is this: While on your life's journey, remember that you have been baptized and you have Jesus at your side. Receive from the tabernacle the bread which can strengthen you for your pilgrim journey. In the gospel we heard about the disciples on the road to Emmaus who, while on the trip, kept their heads hanging. Jesus says to you that he is present to you so that you can grow in hope and love. We hope that for your common journey, you will enjoy his help on good days and bad.

25

Hinge Your Marriage on God

Preparation

A mobile that has been crafted by friends of the bridal couple. Perhaps some elements have special reference to marriage: an anchor (hope), a heart (love), an umbrella (reconciliation), or a dove (peace). Then put in some other appropriate readings!

Readings

Rom 12:9-18: *About intimacy with each other.*
Col 3:12-15: *Love keeps everything together.*
1 Thess 5:15-18: *How we best deal with each other.*
John 15:1-5: *Separated from me you can do nothing (vine and branches)*

The Homily

This mobile which *(name)* has been crafted for you may be hung in your home as a remembrance of this day. The following are some reflections regarding this mobile and its symbolic meaning for you on this wedding day.

    1. You see how the individual components keep mutually in balance. They swing around and twist around each other. We hope for similar harmony for you on your common journey. If that journey is to be successful, it will depend on your interrelationship. Partnership and participation (taking part and permitting the other to take part) means that each is ready to give and take, to take and give. That is not too much for

anyone; behavior of this kind gives mutual support which allows one to tackle problems at home. In that way harmony and good feeling will prevail, even if conflicts are not always avoided.

2. You see in this mobile that all the components are connected, one with the other. The threads which tie them together can be called love or kindness, and security or trust. We have heard what love can mean in Paul's letter to the Romans: "Rejoice in hope, be patient in suffering, persevere in prayer. . . . Rejoice with those who rejoice, weep with those who weep. Live in harmony with one another. . . . Do not repay anyone evil for evil. . . . If it is possible, so far as it depends on you, live peaceably with all" (Rom 12:12-18). Love indeed keeps everything in order. (If the individual pieces are placed too close to one another, there will be clashing.) In that case, only the strings that bind us to each other are left alone. The other party should not pull us by these threads as though we were unwilling marionettes.

3. The various items never hang absolutely still; they are constantly revolving. In your case here today you have not yet arrived in the sure harbor of marriage. Just the opposite; now begins the journey on the open sea. Or, as the Scottish proverb says, "When you get married you get a sealed manuscript, the contents of which you learn when you are out on the open sea." Go out now on your journey of discovery; be prepared to change course on this very unpredictable journey; never say: "Now I know you!" In marriage you need never give up your personality, but in accordance with your *yes* here today, every new discovery and self-realization must be followed in a way that takes into consideration the other party: Hence you need not be always "falling in love," but at the same time you should look commonly in the same direction so as to change with the other person.

4. When a new element is brought into the picture, all the other objects must re-adjust. That can go well only when compromise is possible, when each is ready to change their position a little bit. It begins with genuine hospitality and be-

comes most noticeable when children come along, throwing the entire mobile in all directions.

5. Two smaller items are supported by a larger one. Often, due to rootedness in one's faith at certain times in the life of a couple, one partner is more capable and therefore must assume more responsibility. That can be a burden, but in the long run we will find it to be a gift, and we will be inwardly content only if we give that gift away.

6. Many elements of the mobile spin only around themselves. And, despite that, they are dragged along. You know how tiresome those relatives and friends are who always use things for their own purposes. And still, if despair and sadness are to diminish in our world, even in a small way, we can't cut ourselves off very easily from them. On the whole, as your marriage succeeds, you will be able to put up more with other people. Are you now ready to say *yes* to the question: "Are you ready as Christian people to fulfill your responsibilities in marriage and family, in the Church and in the world?"

7. This mobile must be fastened to a central point on which everything hangs for support. If the unit falls down from this fixed point, then of course all movement ceases. We heard in the gospel, ". . . apart from me you can do nothing" (John 15:5). God is that fixed point in the mobile on whom we depend. The mobile example is similar to a spider which, on a beautiful morning, eases out to improve its web. Often a spider will forget the original purpose of the "ladder" it made to climb up and down its web. Thinking it looks unnecessary, it bites the web, which falls down and entangles the spider. How much suffering could be spared if only people would remember that God is their ladder on the web, or the fixed point of the mobile. It is God who protects us and makes life possible.

Now here you have come today. You are not here for the sake of celebration, but rather to show yourselves ready for marriage. The word "religion" in its root meaning indicates that one allows oneself to be completely held by another. When

I now bind your hands with this stole, which is decorated with the sign of Christ, everyone can be sure that on your common journey you are entrusting yourselves to the first one in your union, the creator and redeemer, who will keep you and us throughout our entire lives.

26

About Little Words

Preparation

For the bridal couple and for each of the participants, one small piece of fur cuttings found in a furrier shop.

Readings

1 Cor 13:4-8a: *What true love can do.*
1 Thess 5:15-18: *Instructions for good interacting.*
1 Pet 3:8-15a: *Exhortation for harmony and good conduct.*
John 15:9-12: *Abide in my love.*

The Homily

I have for you a small piece of fur as a remembrance of this hour. The fur is significant because it is not always the big acts of disloyalty, financial problems, or differences of education that break up marriages in our present times; rather it is the little things: the cap not put back on the tube of toothpaste, and hair left in the sink, any of the seemingly insignificant, routine events of the day. People gathered here in this church today surely can give many examples of such little irritants.

Because of this, I give you both a little piece of fur which you can attach to the mirror in your car or home, or to your clothing so that you can recall the importance of these "small" words. There is a story about a village in which the people, upon meeting each other, always offered a little, warm, soft piece of fur. The fur was symbolic of friendship, attentiveness, a good word, or a smile. And so it was that since each one would pass that on to someone else, the supply never ran out. That changed one day when a disgruntled villager gave this advice: "Now don't be so generous with your little pieces of fur; they're just going to come around back to you anyway!" This calculating advice spoiled everything, for those who were calculating by disposition not only stopped handing out their pieces of fur but they became mistrusting, cynical, sniping, and negative toward others. Eventually they forgot that friendliness and good words usually doubled in value.

What can the little pieces of fur mean for your relationship? It is the "little" words and deeds which show thanks, give praise, cause the other party to laugh, cry, sing, or become peaceful and reflective. When I am able to come to grips with my interior, I am better able to meet my other half once again. In sacred scripture there are many other little "words" which can embellish everyday life in marriage and keep your marriage vital. We heard in the letter of Peter, "Finally, all of you, have unity of spirit, sympathy, love for one another, a tender heart, and a humble mind. Do not repay evil for evil or abuse for abuse. . . . for 'Those who desire life and desire to see good days,/ let them keep their tongues from evil/ and their lips from speaking deceit;/ let them turn away from evil and do good;/ let them seek peace and pursue it . . . do not fear what they fear, and do not be intimidated, but in your hearts sanctify Christ as Lord" (1 Pet 3:8-15a; see also the reference from Cor 13 or 1 Thess 5:15-18). Or "Let your speech be always gracious, seasoned with salt, so that you may know how you ought to answer everyone" (Col 4:6).

Lovely couple! We wish for your marriage a good supply of fur pieces so that, eventually, you can put together a "fur coat" made from the many soft and warm pieces of fur you were given through the years. God will give you the "fur coat" of his goodness. That will be made more clear to you in a special way when I wrap around your clasped hands this stole which is decorated with the symbol of Christ as the good shepherd. "Remain in my love!" Jesus says to you in the gospel just read. Union with him is a guarantee that he will keep your marriage safe in good days and bad. Take these little pieces of fur with you as a memento. Be careful of beginnings! Put into your encounters more heart than hands!

27

About Oil in the Marriage Vessel

Preparation

An oil lamp with wick and oil—an item procurable in an antique shop.

Readings

Col 3:12-15: *Above all else love one another.*
Phil 4:4-9: *Christ-like fundamental attitudes.*
Matt 5:14-16: *You are the light of the world.*
Matt 25:1-13: *The wise bridesmaids carried oil with them.*

The Homily

I would like to give you for your journey in marriage this antique oil lamp and oil container.

In the gospel we just heard about a marriage ceremony. Only the five people who brought oil along in the containers were allowed to celebrate. Thus it is important that you bring sufficient oil with you into the marriage.

A shortage of oil in a lamp causes the wick to burn out quickly. A shortage of oil in a machine causes it to overheat. Oil allows a machine to run coolly and smoothly, just as it allows a lamp to burn brightly and slowly. In terms of a marriage, oil prevents friction through its lubricating qualities.

Mother Teresa of Calcutta one time said that ''The drops of oil in our lamps are the little things in daily life: fidelity, punctuality, little friendly words, a thought about another, our art and manner in keeping silence, in speaking and in acting.'' Paul listed similar virtues in the reading just heard such as heartfelt mercy, kindness, humility, meekness, patience, forgiveness, love, peace, and thankfulness (Col 3:12-15; or Phil 4:4-9).

(Here thanks can be extended to the parents and friends of the couple, for the good relationships with them brought oil into the jars of life which the couple are now to bring with them into the marriage.)

The oil in the lamps is your trust in one another, but it includes putting your security in God, into whose hands you are giving yourselves this day. This will be clearer, now, as I bind your joined hands with this stole inscribed with the sign of Christ. Trust one another and put your security in God who will be your protective covering in the temptations and dangers of your environment. The atmosphere of trust and security provides also the necessary warmth for the nest into which your children must be brought if they are to grow up in sound body and soul.

So it is that we wish for you in your marriage adequate oil in your lamps at all times so that you may be the light of the world (Matt 5:14). Meanwhile your *yes* is needed for the Church and society alike if we are to bring light into the darkness of this world.

You will be questioned about love and the oil in your lamps at the end of your life. Your love for one another and for God will be decisive as to whether you, as the bridesmaids in the gospel story, will have to stand at the door, or whether you will be permitted to enter into the eternal high feast with the Son of God.

Now I will light this oil lamp of yours from the altar candles and then allow it to burn on the altar during this divine service. Perhaps you might light it as a remembrance of this hour on your wedding anniversaries. The wick and the little lamp will provide good light, that is, assuming there is oil in your marriage.

28

About Farsightedness

Preparation

An embroidered picture or knitted wall hanging. Please pick one of these before the wedding in consultation with friends or family.

Readings

Eccl 4:9-12: *A triple-braided cord does not so easily break.*
Cor 13:4-8: *Love resists everything.*
Matt 17:1-9: *On the mountain of the transfiguration for a short time the disciples experienced heaven.*
John 15:9-12: *Abide in my love.*

The Homily

Through this reflection I hope to bless this multicolor, embroidered picture, which I am presenting to you on your wedding day so that it will be for you a special guide on your common journey. Perhaps you can find a place of honor for it in your home.

1. Your marriage is similar to a woven mural, or similar to this embroidered picture. Begin today with this piece of handwork, and add each day a few threads to it. An Eastern metaphor says every person, and every married couple, at the end of life must hand to the Creator a picture that has been worked on throughout one's life. Every happening in life,

whether happy or sad events, good or bad days, must be woven into certain colors so that the final product well represents one's personal or married life. We hope for you that your marriage picture will be a colorful, living pattern of this little work of art.

2. The needle which you use for stitching should be love. It holds everything together. Love can have many names such as kindness, patience, forgiveness, joy, or thankfulness. And if you work with love, it will help you work through the problems of the day. If you remain bound to God in love, he will stay by your side at all times. Today, God watches over while you anchor your love for one another on rock. The stole which I now lay on your hands should express this.

3. Days will come along for you when in the evening you will ask "Why does God allow that?" Is there any justice which punishes these happenings? Is there only mercy for lies? These are difficult questions.

Humans cause much suffering by their misuse of freedom. Inasmuch as God is almighty, he has not reduced us to marionettes. We have the freedom to decide against God and righteousness. In giving us this freedom he has given us a very great gift.

In the end, we cannot ask "why?" but we can ask "for what purpose?" Even Jesus had no answer to the "why?"; that which he could not or would not change, he accepted and so redeemed the world.

And now comes my third point: Look at the back side of this woven picture. Do you see the maze of the threads, the knots, the blurred pattern? Often times in life we see only the back side of a thing which disturbs, threatens, and causes us sadness. After many years, or perhaps at the end of life, we might recognize the beautiful side of the embroidery; where everything once seemed confused, we might find an especially beautiful pattern. Ask older people today. Certainly there are some people right in our midst who can say that, after some years, they were able to see an entirely different pattern than what they previously saw.

4. Today you are beginning to embroider the image of your marriage. The children which we wish for you might become the most beautiful image that you will come to enjoy. Besides children, an open house, a lived hospitality, can bring color and outline to your common journey. Good friends and co-workers—may they all be woven into the work of art of your marriage.

So take this small work of art with you in your marriage so that it may serve to remind you of this joyous event, in good times and in bad.

29

Seek and Protect That Which Is Precious

Preparation

A beautiful half-shell for both partners. (For each of the visitors a shell of which thousands can be found on the beaches.)

Readings

Eccl 4:9-12: *Two are better at things than one.*
Matt 13:45: *The parable of the pearl.*
Matt 19:3-6: *Man and wife become one.*

The Homily

I would like to give each of you a half-shell as a remembrance of this hour of your marriage. Perhaps you can give it a good, safe place in your home so as to serve as a reminder of the thoughts expressed here today.

  1. Isn't this shell a little work of art? How rich nature always is, so much so that millions of these shells lie on the beach. And each one is distinctly different!

  And you, my dear friends, are unchangeably unique and most worthy of love among the multi-millions of small children. We are happy that you have now put the decision process behind you and want to join together the two halves of a shell in order to protect that which is most precious in them.

2. But first of all look at the open half. It is ready to receive and to be filled up. You are now happily awaiting the honeymoon. It is our hope that at the beach or in the mountains you will open your soul to the sun just like this shell so that your inner shell, your interior fountain, can be filled up. That sounds somewhat egotistical, but it is important that you first of all feel good about yourself. You can share as soon as your inner shell is filled. Remember that part of the principal commandment is that "You shall love your neighbor as *yourself.*" You must first of all have this feeling of self worthiness, to say *yes* to yourself as you are—with your talents and your inadequacies. You will need time, even in the twosomeness of marriage, to find yourself always anew as a person. So become first of all a partner who can part with something from your shell, a partner who is truly an opposite, not only a shadow or a leech. True partnership is only possible in giving and taking, taking and giving, for not everyone has his or her shell completely filled.

3. In marriage you put together your two half-shells as is indicated in the Gospel of Matthew: "So they are no longer two, but one flesh. Therefore what God has joined together, let no one separate" (Matt 19:6). The two halves of the shell must be glued together, so that the precious contents of the shell remain secure and protected.

But partners change and grow. Many partners commit to a marriage contract before times of major personality change. And, because of the so-called self-fulfillment ethic which is so popular in the cultures of the West, such change on the part of the individual is modeled and highly encouraged. Thus, the partners easily go in separate directions and drift apart so much that, in time, their half-shells no longer fit together. This is to say nothing against self-fulfillment— that individuals should give up their personal development after marriage. But, after marriage, your personal development is done in a way that takes into account another—that of your spouse—which redirects or qualifies our individual growth.

4. Please use your imagination and try to picture a small pearl in your shell. A precious pearl starts really from a mishap when a sharp grain of sand gets into the soft part of a shell. That can be deadly! In self-defense against the painful intruder, the shell builds layers upon layers of coating around the grain of sand which, over time, becomes a precious pearl. Of course the lesson here is that from what is burdensome and painful can come something as precious as pearls. I emphasize this, for today we are compelled to rid ourselves of that which is burdensome or unpleasant. Of course I would never wish unpleasant or burdensome things upon your marriage, but a certain amount of trial and tribulation is inevitable. It is most likely that somewhere along your journey, you will encounter hardships. Such hardships are less likely to become major catastrophes, however, if you see them the way a shell sees a grain of sand—that is, something to transform from that which is an intrusion to that which is precious. In other words, from suffering, healing can also come. Today, in this sacrament of marriage, you are beginning a union with God. We have learned that, through Jesus, suffering and even death do not have the last word; rather, such suffering is the beginning of a completely different reality.

5. I urge you to seek the precious pearl of life referred to in the gospel we just heard. Jesus, our guide, whom we know is at our side in good times and in bad, is really the worthwhile pearl for which we give everything else away. We hope that you will continue this search for the precious pearl. The shell should remind you of this.

30

About Dreams and the Good End

Preparation

A kaleidoscope.

Readings

Song of Solomon 8:6-7: *Love keeps all things together.*
1 Cor 13:4-8a: *True love makes all things possible.*
Matt 17:1-9: *The transfiguration of Jesus.*
John 15:9-12: *Abide in my love.*

The Homily

As you begin your journey into marriage, I would like to give you this toy. The word *kaleidoscope* is a combination of several Greek words: "beautiful," the word *eidos,* which means "picture," and the word *skopein,* which means "to look at." Thus, literally, kaleidoscope means to "look at a beautiful picture."

1. Dreams are important. I chose this theme so that you do not forget about dreams in your marriage. We need dreams in order to make room for imagination and energy. I am not talking about daydreams which often merely distract us from reality. I refer to dreams which can become reality, just as you so many times have dreamt about this very hour, which has now become reality. There are in fact many dreams that come to all of us, whether they be that of owning our own home, a new vocation or career, health, loving children, and,

87

naturally, the success of our marriage. We wish for you today the fulfillment of these dreams; later we will ask you about
your future dreams and will pray for them.

Relax! Every day you will need some time for play and
recreation. The bow of the daily routine cannot always be
pulled back too far, otherwise one day it will break, or its tension will be lost. It is in this way that this beautiful toy can
help. Enjoy the beautiful images of the kaleidoscope. You need
quiet time and solitude which is something different from iso-
lation and loneliness. Those who are always on the go, who
have spread themselves too thinly, lose the ability to notice the
little things, and lose the ability to talk and listen. This is the
way cracking begins in the foundation of the marriage building.

A sense of self-worth is also important; even in times of
crisis you will need to be able to say *yes* to yourself as a person. Note that the principal commandment mandates that you
love God and your neighbor as you love yourself. This self
love which we need can diminish gradually, however. And
so we must say *yes* to ourself so as to create the condition which
allows us to love God and neighbor. And those who say *no*
to themselves, in effect, make God responsible for their un-
happiness.

3. If you take this kaleidoscope completely apart so as to
see what makes up the beautiful images in it, one would find
only broken pieces of colorful crystal, wire, and mirrors. It
is hard to imagine how from such a collection of debris can
come such beauty.

You can never know what marriage will bring. Perhaps
there will be moments in which all you see is chaos, nothing
but debris and fragments scattered about. When these moments come, I ask that you "look at a beautiful picture," that
is, put yourself in the hands of a God who will collect all the
broken pieces and put them together into a beautiful image.
He has shown this in his Son who, by the presumed disaster
on the cross, broke down the barriers to another world. Perhaps for the first time after his death, we see that God's ways
are founded on other laws. Often we learn only after many

years how, in everything, hope and understanding accidently come together along the way. Take along strong faith with you into the marriage. This God who makes his way with you gives us his Son as the guide on the journey. That will be clear when your hands are wrapped in this stole which is a symbol of Jesus Christ. ''Remain in my love!'' Jesus told us in the happy message read to you. We pray that on good and bad days you will stay close to Jesus Christ who will bring all things to a good end.

31

About a Firm Foothold

Preparation

A ceramic wagon wheel.

Readings

1 John 4:16b-21: *Abide in love.*
Matt 22:35-40: *Love of God and neighbor (the principal commandment).*
John 15:1-5: *Abide in me, then I will abide in you (vine and branches).*

Comment

Please make a choice!

The Homily

This is a ceramic wagon wheel which I present to you as a remembrance of this hour of your marriage. Please put it in a special place in your home. When you look at it, call to mind, then, one of the following thoughts:

    1. In order to be a spoke in the wheel—and all of us are spokes in the wheel of the work-a-day world, country, and Church—the corner and edges of this wood must fit together. If, at the beginning in your marriage, the wheel is not spinning smoothly, then you must allow the other to change you—to adjust the spokes of the wheel—so that it might turn

smoothly. Without a genuine openness to change, real growth cannot happen.

2. Each spoke needs a center, the hub, which holds and directs it. As we have just heard in the gospel, the center for us Christians is God who, in Christ, put his Son in our midst. If we allow ourselves to be anchored in Christ, we will remain bound to him and have a firm foothold on good and bad days. Anyone who is moved off center can be tossed about as the wheel spins.

3. The nearer the spokes get to the center, the closer they are to each other. In terms of the sacrament of marriage this means that, as you confer the sacrament of marriage on each other—the priest is only the ecclesiastical witness—you come ever closer to Jesus. Every time your love flows back and forth, you come as close to Christ as you did at the reception of Holy Communion. In the image of the wagon wheel, you can better understand the mystery of the Eucharist: in receiving Holy Communion we are joined with Christ and with each other.

4. The spokes also need the support and the connection with the outside to the rim. Love of God in the same way extends out to love of neighbor. You cannot take permanent refuge only in the companionship of marriage; that quickly amounts to imprisonment. You need others such as friends and relatives. Notice that your closest relations are placed around you in a semi-circle at the wedding ceremony, as if to say they are the next section of the spokes which eventually connect with the rim, and which symbolizes the whole social circle that holds us together and gives us strength.

5. The iron ring around the rim gives added strength, support, and protection. I could say much about how the little wheel of your wedding protects you. But the most important thing, however, is your love, loyalty, and trust in each other. In German this celebration is called a *trauung* which loosely is translated as "trusting one another." For the protection of your marriage, moreover, forgiving kindness is needed, a willingness for peace shown by such little words as "thank you," "I love you," and "I can't live without you." If this

ring around the rim remains intact, then the wheel will run right over all the little stones you come upon in your journey through life.

6. Very often the wheel gets stuck in a quagmire of problems. It is then that you will need good friends with whom you can spend a bit of your free time; you will also need the help of Christians to give support on the journey. Those of us who are here today hope that you will not be disappointed by us in our assisting you in your difficulties.

7. For the wheel to remain intact, you must say *yes* now to children. Children are new spokes who stabilize the wheel; at the same time they will give support and meaning to your life.

I am happy to bind your joined hands with this stole, which bears the image of Christ, so that you remain firmly centered in the hub of Christ from whom we just heard in the gospel: "Abide in me as I abide in you" (John 15:4).

32

About Fidelity

Preparation

A rosebush for planting.

Readings

Rom 13:8-10: *We are always indebted to love.*
1 Cor 13:4-8a: *About the Canticle of Love.*

The Homily

I would like to present to you this rosebush to plant in your garden. If it gets old and gnarled, all that is necessary is to cut off a shoot, put it in the ground and watch it sprout anew. It is symbolic of renewed love. From this rosebush you can always cut off three roses to remind you of what I will now say.

Every now and then you will ask your partner as Jesus did in the gospel: "Do you love me?" Peter became concerned after being asked the question the third time as it implied doubt on the part of Jesus. (In his gospel, St. John seems to connect the threefold question with the threefold denial of Peter recorded three chapters earlier.)

Permit me to pose three questions:

1. Imagine your present love as a rose—radiant, tender, and sweet smelling—and that your love were to ask you a question. Surely, your answer would gush forth. After all, this is your wedding day, your time of celebration.

2. Imagine the rose, now, with sharp-edged thorns that pierce. Suppose your partner were to have an accident in

which he or she were rendered unconscious, or were to suddenly become very cool and distant from you. Such things can even be worse than death, as you must still deal with this person even though they are much different from the person you married.

3. And now imagine the third rose from this rosebush; it is withered away, but surrounded by all that which is left behind, perhaps with great grandchildren on the shoot. And then the question is asked: "Do you still have love for me when my spirits and energies are so weakened? Do you love me all the time, even when I am so withered?"

You notice that true love is more than some weakly muttered "I love you." You heard in the gospel just read "[love] bears all things, believes all things, hopes all things, endures all things" (1 Cor 13:7-8). Such love surpasses our human powers many times, which is the reason we are here. For whoever puts themselves in God's hands, lives by God's love, is empowered to practice fidelity until death. Now put your hands together as a sign of your love and trust in each other. Please put this stole, a sign of Christ, around your hands. Remember that Christ will be with you in good times and in bad. In God your good plans and energies are anchored as long as you are willing to remain bound to him. As John writes of Christ in his gospel "Abide in me as I abide in you. Just as the branch cannot bear fruit by itself unless it abides in the vine, neither can you unless you abide in me" (John 15:4-5).

It is also very significant that the risen Christ, prior to his crucial question, first celebrated the Eucharistic service with Peter and the other apostles: "Jesus came and took the bread and gave it to them. . ." (John 21:13). By that action we were then, as we are today, united with, and therefore empowered by, Christ.

So allow yourselves now to be united with God and Christ. And may this rosebush, which I hope some day your children will enjoy, produce for you many fragrant, tender roses.

33

Healing

Preparation

A colorful bouquet with some healing herbs.

Readings

Col 3:12-15: *Healing herbs for the marriage.*
John 15:9-12: *Abide in my love.*

The Homily

Once again today we are discovering the powers of nature. With that in mind I am giving you as a symbol for your common journey this little bundle of healing herbs so that your marriage can be healthy in body and soul. Perhaps you can hang this up somewhere safely in your home to remind you of this day.

1. It could happen that sometime you might fall into a depression at the loss of employment, when you can't seem to understand one another, or when emptiness creeps into your marriage. In the case of depression the healing herb, mistletoe, is helpful.

Paul mentions the healing herb of thankfulness in this last reading (Col 3:15b). Remain thankful for the partner who has been given to you. Learn how to be thankful for the little things; such people do not hanker around, envious of what others have. Such dissatisfaction creates walls and sadness of heart that is destructive to any marriage.

2. Continuous aggravations at work can lead to disorders of the stomach which naturally have repercussions in the marriage and family. Liquorice roots are valued for their healing quality of quieting people down.

In Paul's first letter to the Corinthians, we find an example of another healing herb—that of bearing with one another (13:4-7). This can also mean to bring an end to aggravations and the demands brought from outside the marriage.

3. In the case of wounds, the healing herb, ribgrass, is helpful even for wasp stings. Here, one may call to mind all the routine wounds and the little hurts we suffer such as the wasp stings of irony and criticism.

Paul points to humility—the courage to be of service. The individual who puts the partner on a higher level than oneself will never be in danger of offending.

4. Frequently a thunderstorm clears the air in a marriage. In case you have bellowed out heatedly in this situation, the healing herb, elderberry, is useful. Paul praises kindness, the friendliness of the heart. A brawl is more easily avoided by the use of this healing herb, even in the heat of misunderstandings which often arise.

5. Partners often complain that the other doesn't pay adequate attention in a conversation. This can be due to stress and agitation which brings on a decrease in concentration. This can be helped by the Chinese healing herb of ginseng (*panax schinseng*) which has five foliated leaves, scarlet berries, and an aromatic root valued for its medicinal purposes.

Paul recommends meekness when a marriage partner no longer perceives the heartbeat of the other partner. Meekness has the effect of bringing about self-forgetfulness, which relieves tension in the other.

6. Hops also have the value of relieving tension. But what has brought about the tension? Are there too many tasks that you have undertaken? Are your goals too many and too high? Have you taken on too many responsibilities so that nothing is any longer done correctly?

Paul praises peace as a healing herb in marriage. To achieve that I must also say *no* to many things.

7. Children, which we wish for you, often get noisy and can cause headaches. To counteract this, balm, known as Melissa, is helpful.

Paul has confidence in the healing herb, joy, which widens the heart so that tension can't take root.

8. When the children act out, digestive troubles often beset us. For this I recommend gentian (the rhizome and roots of a yellow-flowered gentian of southern Europe are used as a tonic and stomachic to relieve headaches).

Paul encourages compassion and kind-heartedness as the response to commotion, but these virtues have not been cultivated in our time. In these situations, harshness won't help but a sympathetic heart will.

9. When your marriage comes into danger and a cold sweat keeps you from sleeping at night, I recommend valerian (a drug consisting of the dried rootstock and roots of the garden heliotrope, formerly used as a sedative).

Paul speaks of a biblical herb, "forgive one another." It induces a new beginning which can work wonders.

10. Anyone in a marriage who does not take fidelity seriously and who casts many side glances, should not be surprised about having lumbago, which is a kind of rheumatism of the loins. But an antibody for this is St. John's wort (any of the genus of herbs and shrubs with showy, pentamerous, and yellow flowers should work).

In the gospel message we heard the words of Jesus: "Keep the commandments!" With this healing herb in which discipline is to be found, I will stay on the right road. Adultery begins already by entertaining thoughts. For that reason we have the directive, "Keep the commandments" which reaches into our thoughts and words.

11. We are not wishing it for you, but it is possible that happenings may come upon you such as sickness or death of a loved one, which can bring with them heaviness of heart. For this condition I prescribe a spring-flowering spirea.

Obviously no herb exists as a tonic against death or the sadness at the loss of a loved one. Nevertheless, Paul recommends perseverance—the ability to stand strong through difficult times. For many misfortunes, it is only after some time that we will be able to understand the meaning behind such events.

12. This last healing herb, garlic, sounds somewhat banal, but it works. A person who regularly, from childhood on, takes it, it has been shown, lives longer and with more vigor. I recommend that you take it with parsley and curd at breakfast. Of course, garlic has a strong side effect, which can keep you for the entire day at arm's length from much temptation, thereby allowing you to be faithful in your marriage.

There is another very effective healing herb which operates on another level: the bible calls it love, which is an herb that allows one to suffer all things (1 Cor 13:4-8a). Love brought you together; it can also heal you again. As Jesus says in the gospel: ''Love one another as I have loved you'' (John 15:12). Because God loves us, we are able to pass love on. There is no *must* or *should* here, but a continual flowing of divine love through you down to your children and out to every human. For Paul, love is that which links everything together in perfect harmony (Col 3:14).

The band of love, which holds all things together, lies around these healing herbs. The band of the love of God, which is symbolized by this stole here, is decorated with the sign of Jesus. With it I now bind your enjoined hands.

We wish for you that you will live your life in the safety vessel of God's love so that you will be kept intact and afloat on good and bad days.

34

About Healing Water

Preparation

Perhaps you might encourage the grandparents to present as a gift a little holy water font, if it should not be too costly.

Readings

1 John 4:16b-19: *Abide in love.*
John 15:1-5: *Abide united with me (vine and branches).*
John 15:9-12: *Abide in my love.*

The Homily

If I did not know the depth of your Christian faith, I would have made myself a laughing stock with this present of a holy water font that *(name)* is giving you. I would be happy if you will hang it in, or close by, your bedroom and make a habit of doing the following:

1. Before you fall exhausted into bed, make a conscious Sign of the Cross with holy water and recall some appeasing words. Even if you have been punished after some conflict by icy silence, which can happen in the best of marriages, do not neglect to say "good night." Perhaps you have more than once been kept awake at night by a cold sweat. We wash away the sweat of the day from our face before we go to sleep. Likewise, we should do the same with our soul, which will allow us pleasant dreams. The soul needs our help when it falls into the unconsciousness of sleep (a state into

which our intellect and our will do not slip) in order to rest freely. Hence, like the oil and sweat on your face, wash away the rage and intransigence of the day, otherwise the spiritual fine-tuning will be left undone overnight. A crucifix that is deliberately placed over us is like an evening prayer; it is an act of binding ourselves with God, our center; it is placing ourselves in God's hands. It is like the action whereby I now place your joined hands in this stole which is decorated with the sign of Christ. Jesus Christ is the first in your union. In the gospel it says "Abide in me as I abide in you" (John 15:4). The power for this reconciliation with a partner and with one's own soul stems from this union and streams out from the crucifix.

2. A day with a peaceful attitude, of course, will go better than a day in which you are angry. For that reason you should get into the habit of starting each day by making consciously and slowly the sign of the cross. Think of it as a short morning prayer, one that gives you a proper attitude as you begin the new day.

3. At both times, morning and evening, the holy water can remind you of your baptism. Baptism was the plunging into God[1] and when you bless yourself you are present again at that moment of baptism. Thus God accepts you just as you are, so that you, plunged into his love, can live happily through faith, hope, and love.

It is a good custom to take some holy water with you from the church. Just as baptism plunged us into the community of Christians, your making your way to church shows us once again your union with the parish community and with the source of all life, Jesus Christ himself.

4. Water gives life. All life comes from water. In fact, we came from the amniotic fluid of our mother's womb, and water flows through us until death. Water is more than bread. Without nourishment we can live several weeks; but without water

---

[1]The German word for Baptism, *Taufe,* comes from the German verb *tauchen,* which means to plunge into water.

we can hardly live ten days. If this water is signed with a cross, there is a special blessing put on it, much like the blessings on your rings which I sprinkled with holy water in the name of Jesus.

So it is our wish for you that when you are in the vicinity of this holy water fountain, you will recall the power of the one who wants to be with you, as long as you want to be bound by him.

35

What Binds Together

Preparation

This homily is for a silver jubilee celebration. As in the case of all the homilies in this book, however, it can be adjusted for use at either silver or golden celebrations. For it you will need a large paper clasp.

Readings

1 Cor 13:4-8a, 13: *But now there remain faith, hope, and love.*
John 15:9-12: *Love in order that my joy may be in you.*

The Homily

I would like to present to you this paper clasp as a remembrance of this day as you journey on in life. You see, it consists of two parts which are held together by a spring. If this spring in the middle fails to work, both of the parts fall apart.

Do you remember the spark that was ignited in you upon meeting each other? Soon after you began noticing how unique and special the other was to you, which of course was the beginnings of love. This romantic love is symbolized by the first spring in this paper clasp which held you together.

After some weeks or months, perhaps, the intuition grew that this other could be your partner for life. The word for "marriage" in German is very meaningful in that it translates as "trusting one another." In considering marriage, you made an act of trust—in yourself that you could love another for life, and in another, that they could do the same for you.

After trusting yourself to love, hope became the next concern in that you hoped to love for a lifetime. Then one day you came before the altar, not so much because there was to be a big celebration in the church or because you belonged to the Church, but because you wanted to make the clasp even stronger. The meaning of the sacrament of marriage became clearer when you extended your hands and the priest wrapped them in his stole which is decorated with the figure of Christ. God at the same moment put his hands around your hands to keep them together so that your hope would not dwindle with the passage of time. Those who put God first in their marriage enjoy the power of God's love at work in their relationship.

As we heard in the readings, it has been faith, hope, and love which has kept you together these last twenty-five years. And you see then that, if the clasp is tightly fastened, many things can be bound together. This is the same for your children, who gain a feeling of security and support from the love, hope, and faith which is at the heart of their parent's relationship. But how many difficulties await the children who come forth from a marriage in which this clasp has become loose or has broken altogether? This would include your many friends, who enjoy the hospitality and warmth from your relationship as well. And if you are truly bound together, any adversity you experience will, in the end, strengthen your marriage.

It is our wish for you today that you will continue to feel the power of this clasp and that your loyalty to your partner and to God gives encouragement to many others who are on this journey. If you will now extend your right hands, I will wrap this stole around them which should make you think back to your wedding day as you renew your marriage vows:

May the Lord, our God, tighten evermore the marriage bond which you made twenty-five years ago in his presence and that of the Church. All of you who have gathered here

I take as witnesses to this holy bond. "What God has joined together, let no one separate."

This clasp, which I will give to you at the end of the celebration, I will now place on the altar. May it remind you of the continued faith, hope, and love that sustains you throughout your married lives.

36

Remain United with God

Preparation

A ceramic piece with two sheafs of grain or something to be hung up that was fashioned from the sheafs of grain.

Readings

1 John 4:16b-19: *Abide in love.*
John 15:1-5: *Remain bound to me (vine and branches).*
John 15:9-12: *Abide in my love.*

The Homily

This small ceramic piece of art work, which is soon to adorn your home, shows two sheafs of grain. When you look at it, may it recall for you this day and what was said about these two sheafs.

There is a story of two brothers which I would like to tell you. The younger was married and had children, while the older was unmarried and lived alone. Both of them worked the fields together and harvested the crops together. When it came time to deliver the sheafs to market, they divided them in halves, one bundle for each to carry.

When night came, each one laid down on his bundle of sheafs in order to get to sleep. The older brother however could not get to sleep and said to himself: "My brother has a family, whereas I am all alone and without children and I have taken as many sheafs as he. That is not right." He got up, took some of his sheafs and secretly and softly arranged them in his brother's bundle. A short time later, the young brother woke up and he was likewise thinking of his brother and said to himself: "My brother is alone and has no children. Who is going to take care of him in his old age?" And then he got up and took some of the sheafs from his bundle and lugged them secretly and quietly to the bundle of his older brother. When the brothers got up as day came, they were astonished that their bundles of sheafs were exactly as they were the night before. But neither of them said a word.

On the following night each one waited a little bit until he was sure the other was asleep, at which time each got up and took their sheafs from his own pile to put them on the pile of the other. At midpoint they suddenly met one another and each recognized how good it was that the other was thinking about him. With that they let their sheafs fall and embraced one another in heartfelt love.

My point in telling you this story is that God in heaven looked down and said "Holy, holy may this place be for me. Here I want to live among humans."

You too are now entering holy land, for this love that bound the brothers together is the same love that binds you. In marriage, your attitude toward the other should be like that of each brother—that is, one that desires to make the other party happy. Only in this way can the common journey succeed. But this view of love includes compromise, self-renunciation, and devotion to the other; this kind of love supports you mutually like the sheafs in this little vignette.

"God *is* love, and those who abide in love," as we heard in the reading, "abide in God, and God abides in them" (1 John 4:16b). This is the kind of love in which God dwells. Please join your hands so that I might wrap and fasten them together in this stole, a symbol of God. All of us here pray that you might remain in this love, for in that way nothing can separate you from God—that his love will surround and protect you.

Permit me now to pronounce over you the blessing of God which St. Patrick of Ireland is supposed to have composed:

> May the Lord be before you,
> to show you the correct way.
> May the Lord be near you
> to embrace you in his arms,
> to protect you against dangers.
> May the Lord be behind you,
> to protect you against the treacheries of the evil one.
> May the Lord be beneath you
> to pull you up when you fall.
> May the Lord be in you
> to comfort you when you are sad.
> May the Lord shelter you like a protecting wall,
> when others seduce you.
> May the Lord be over you,
> to bless you.
> May the good Lord bless you
> today, tomorrow and always.

37

Concerning Light in Darkness

Preparation

A richly decorated candle. If it should turn out to be costly, ask some of the relatives or acquaintances in advance to put money together to offer it as a present.

Readings

Song of Solomon 8:6-7: *Mighty waters cannot extinguish the flames of love.*
Matt 5:14-16: *You are the light of the world.*

The Homily

In many households I have found the following quotation framed and hung: "Just at that moment when you've given up hope in starting a fire, a little flame flickers."

It is for this reason that I am handing you this beautiful candle as a present from (*name*), so that from time to time you can light it as a remembrance of this day. On days of personal darkness or sadness you will need to look into the flames of this candle.

1. There is a story of a man who, after a strenuous pilgrimage to a holy place, acquired a flaming torch from which he expected some luck to bring home with him. En route someone in need of warmth asked him if he could start the wood on fire. At first he hesitated, not wanting to use his sacred flame for such a worldly occasion; but in the end he con-

sented, and then was on his way again. As he went on, however, he encountered a bad storm. Though he tried to protect his light from the rain, the flame eventually went out. At this point he fondly remembered the one with whom he shared his light.

Like this man in the story, you have in your lifetime shared your torch. Moreover, like him, you are not standing alone at the beginning of your life's journey. Your family and your closest friends are standing around you at this wedding ceremony. By their presence they are saying that they can be counted on to be with you now, just as they have in the past. Warm fires are burning around those with whom you shared your fire of love, friendship, and attention. And these are people to whom you can return at those times when you need your own fire rekindled.

2. Also, please think back on your baptismal candle, at which time Jesus took you by the hand. I will wrap around your joined hands this stole which bears the image of Jesus Christ. At this point he will be even more in your midst—he who once said, "I am the light of the world. Whoever follows me will never walk in darkness but will have the light of life" (John 8:12). Or, as it says at the beginning of John's Gospel, "The light shines in the darkness. . . ." (John 1:5a).

And, indeed, on the principal feasts of the church year, this light gives streams of light. At Christmas time we celebrate the fact that, in Jesus, light came into the world of darkness. At Easter time the light of the risen Christ becomes the alpha and the omega of our faith; and at Pentecost we think of the fire of God as a force which can open all the tightly locked doors of anxiety.

3. There is still a third possibility for finding "a little light" on gloomy days by doing something for yourself. Marriage counsellors say that an inadequate feeling of self-worth is the reason for many crises. Occasionally we must spend a day visiting ourselves. This is done by spending a few minutes alone, taking a walk, nap, or bath, or by visiting someone for whom things are a bit more distressing. A good conver-

sation with someone who will listen can also be very helpful. For only when I can say *yes* to myself and my situation will I be able to say *yes* again to my neighbor and to God. It is better to light a light than to curse the darkness. And the entire darkness of the world is not capable of putting out this little light of yours.

So take this beautiful candle as a memento of this day with you into your marriage and, from time to time, recall from where this comforting ''little light'' came, should darkness someday surround you. We wish for you good friends, new strength from your trust in Jesus, and the discovery as to how valuable each of you is to us as members of the church and citizens of this nation.

38

On the Common Expedition

Preparation

Have on hand a beautiful walking stick, or possibly two. In case it gets to be too expensive, a joint purchase by relatives or a traveling organization might make it more affordable.

Readings

Ps 23: *The Lord is my shepherd; his staff gives me confidence.*
Eccl 4:9-12: *Two are better at it than one alone.*
Luke 24:13-35: *On the road to Emmaus.*
John 14:1-6: *I am the way.*
John 15:1-5: *Abide in me.*

The Homily

I wish to give you this beautiful walking stick for your common journey as a married couple. Yes, life is like an expedition, even for married people. Since you like to travel, this can often remind you of your wedding day and the thoughts which I wish to share with you today. Here are four thoughts—like the four points of the compass.

1. As man and woman, you are already on a common journey in which you look ahead in the same direction. The issue is no longer one of romantic love, but one of shared vision. Just as up to this point you wanted still to consider yourselves as individual persons and personalities, so today, after your *yes,* each of you must redirect your future steps toward

the other so that you do not drift away from one another or pass out of sight on the next turn of the road.

2. What persons and places will you encounter? Will you encounter more rain or more sunshine? The number, the position of the persons, or the beauty of the places is not important; what is of most importance is how you encounter them.

Whomever you meet at the moment is the most important. It is the stretch of road just before you each day that is the most important. Indeed the most important day is always today. And the most important deed on all expeditions is always to seek the good. In that way, whether in rain or shine, it makes no difference because you have love in your hearts. Everything you thought you wasted altruistically has a way of coming back to you as good.

3. On steep roads a walking stick is a good support staff, for the heart will not have to pump so hard when climbing, and it relieves the knees on the downward tread. Hopefully the Church will serve as a support staff for you on your journey. You have come here to this church today to say your *yes* in the presence of God and this church. It is the Church which gives you God's blessing, and it is the Church who gives witness to the one who will walk with you, and to the one who is in our midst. Faith in Jesus and the Church is like a staff in your hands, as the Psalmist said some three thousand years ago: "Even though I walk through the darkest valley,/ I fear no evil;/ for you are with me;/ your rod and your staff—they comfort me" (Ps 23:4-5).

4. In the gospel we heard about the disciples on the road to Emmaus. It is one of the most beautiful and striking gospel passages for, in the midst of their sadness and disappointment, they felt the presence of Jesus in their hearts once again. Jesus, who appeared in their midst, is recognized only as they rested in the village for a bite to eat. This same Jesus will also go with you as long as you wish to remain bound to him. This will now become clearer to you as I envelop your hands with this stole which is decorated with the symbol of Jesus Christ. He will stay with you and guide you on good and bad days.

5. There are four points on the compass, just as you have listened to my four thoughts. Number five is the number of the living, the number at the marriage, because the representatives in your wedding party consist of two from the female side, the bride and bride's maid, and three from the male side, the groom, the best man, and the minister. And from that consideration comes our fifth point: In many cultures there are five points of the compass, one pointing in each direction and the fifth pointing to ourselves. Each individual is also the center point of his or her own world; it is critical to make the journey inward so that, above all, our heart can be a dwelling place for God. Consequently, those who truly want to love their spouse on the journey to their common goal, must first of all find their own, innermost being, have a feeling of self-worth, be able to say *yes* to oneself, with all one's positives and negatives. For it is only then that one is truly able to meet the other. Also it may be good to sometimes travel together in silence so each of you can come to terms with yourselves, the world, and God. In other words, go inside yourself so that you can come entirely out of yourself.

You see, this walking stick can be of much help on your common journey. And now I would like to bind you with Jesus, your guide on the journey, who says "Those who abide in me and I in them bear much fruit . . . ." (John 15:5).

39

The Sacred Number Seven

Preparation

With the help of a close relative or co-worker of the couple—especially a party who has celebrated a silver anniversary of marriage—arrangements can be made for someone to purchase a seven-branch candlestick as a wedding gift for the bride and groom.

Readings

1 Cor 13:4-8a, 13: *Now there remain faith, hope, and love.*
Matt 18:21-22: *How often must I forgive my partner?*

The Homily

This beautiful, seven-branch candlestick is a present from *(name)* which will surely have a special place in your heart because today, on your wedding day, in this homily, it is given a special place of honor. Perhaps you can light it up on your anniversaries as a remembrance of this day.

In Judaism, the seven-branch candlestick is a holy sign. But I am thinking now more about the sacred number seven, the number commonly indicating abundance and perfection.

1. Today you are administering to each other the sacrament of matrimony, which is seventh in the list of sacraments which we accept in the Catholic faith. And, if you permit the fullness of grace to flow into you, you will be able to go with trust in God more easily on your common journey. All of us

here wish you will feel as though you are in "seventh heaven"—on your common journey.

2. Every seven years the body renews itself, but there is nothing more added to the body than it previously had. But you must pledge yourselves to renewing each other's body and spirit beyond that seventh year, for our loyalty must be like God's—that is, eternal.

3. The rainbow, which is a symbol of reconciliation between God and humankind, has seven colors. We heard in the gospel that a brother, sister, or partner must be forgiven at least seven times. But for Christians, our readiness to forgive should never cease. The power to do this can be procured only from faith.

4. There are also the seven gifts of the Holy Spirit, which we all wish for you in your marriage: The gift of wisdom—that is, the knowledge which is so important in life, for great knowledge is not crucial; the gift of understanding, which is to understand everything properly, to see everything with the heart, and to see the finger of God behind every happening; the gift of counsel, which is to accept good advice, but also good-naturedly to give advice; the gift of knowledge which is to know oneself and one's limitations, to say *yes* to oneself so as to be able to know in a real way the other partner; and the gift of fortitude which is the courage to act on one's convictions. Considered together with these are courage and perseverance, which allow us to swim occasionally against the tide and the "ways of the world." The gift of piety is also important, as it is the gift which allows us to see, finally, that everything is gift. And, finally, I wish for you the gift of fear of God, which speaks of the reverence—that combination of honor and fear—needed to love God.

5. Also we wish for you the seven virtues which consist of the three divine virtues—that of faith, hope, and love—and the four cardinal virtues: prudence, justice, fortitude, and temperance.

6. In the symbolic language of the bible, it states that God rested on the seventh day of the week. The seven day rhythm

of the week seems to be incorporated into the body, perhaps because of the phases of the moon which last seven days. There is a naturalness to taking rest on the seventh day. This is why I discourage you from working on all seven days, which can diminish your ability to hear your inner voice and the heart beat of the other party. And of course an important part of that day is our common worship of God in the community of Christians, which reminds us that we can be hopeful as we have been redeemed through the resurrection of Christ.

7. Finally, as we think about the number seven, we recall the seven sorrows of Mary which also may await you. Even in moments when your soul seems pierced by a sword, life—including married life—must go on. There are also the seven joys of Mary and the crises revolving around the child Jesus, whose coming had been announced by a seven-pointed comet. This same Jesus offers you his help and his guidance on your journey. Each of you will be able to see this when this stole, decorated as it is with the image of Christ, is now wrapped around your joined hands. It will keep you on good days and bad.

So now take this seven-branch candlestick with you into your marriage. It can say a great deal to you as you journey on your common way.

40

Latch on to Happiness

Preparation

A stepladder will be needed. Here relatives and acquaintances of the bridal couple might jointly acquire this exciting gift for presentation at the time of the wedding homily. An alternative would be a handcrafted imaginative "bird of paradise."

Readings

Eccl 4:9-12: *Two are better than one alone.*
Col 3:12-15: *Above all things, love one another.*
Matt 20:25-28: *Serve and don't rule.*
John 15:1-5: *Abide in me.*

The Talk

This stepladder, the gift of *(name)* to you, lovely couple, is to be the central point of the homily. This is because in your marriage you will often be climbing a high ladder, in terms of career, children, and your marriage. The following are some suggestions to help you in this climb.

1. Partnership means learning how to balance. The higher one climbs up a ladder, the less stable things become. For that reason the other should be standing by to give the partner a sure hand. Both must in a sense stay with one another so that the one on the ladder does not fall. The security of a stable ladder is needed if each partner is to feel safe enough to assume the responsibility of marriage and family.

In public life one can stand much higher than the other, but not at the expense of the other party. This is something to which the other partner must also agree. Be ready to give and to take, to take and to give. There is no such thing as superior and subordinate, even when I am standing below and am holding the ladder. Your complementarity enriches you. To clarify roles, continuous communication is essential.

2. Theologian Martin Buber tells a story of a bird of paradise in which a beautifully colored, exotic bird—the bird of paradise—was perched on the branch of a tree. The inhabitants knew that if they captured it, the city would remain in fate's good favor. And so with joy they decided to build a living ladder. Just when the last person had completed his work and wanted to seize the "bringer of luck," the strength of the lowest person in the string of persons failed, thus causing all to tumble to the ground. The bird, of course, remained uncaptured.

I would like to share with you this thought regarding your marriage which you no doubt hope will bring you good luck and satisfaction: "Paradise" is an interesting word, for, at least in marriage, no such thing can be found. Unfortunately, some easily exaggerate their hopes of their marriage, and thus are necessarily led to disappointment; where they are expecting a "bird of paradise," they get a grey house sparrow. Hence, the ladder to success in marriage cannot depend on dreams but needs a firm foundation on what is real so as not to be destroyed. The ladder needs one who climbs up on it and one who holds it for support. One alone cannot hold together the "we."

You can discover what this togetherness, which you must try on a daily basis, is like in the reading: "As God's chosen ones, holy and beloved, clothe yourselves with compassion, kindness, humility, meekness, and patience. Bear with one another and if anyone has a complaint against another, forgive each other just as the Lord has forgiven you. Above all, clothe yourselves with love which binds everything in perfect harmony" (Col 3:12-14).

3. Interestingly, in many of the pictures showing the stable in Bethlehem and the cross of Calvary there is a ladder. In this way the artist wanted to express that Jesus, as the Son of God, used the ladder to climb down to earth from heaven to become man. Likewise, Jesus joins us in this marriage ceremony by becoming a companion to you on your marriage journey. And, of course, along the way he will have many important things to say to us such as ". . . whoever wishes to be great among you must be your servant" (Matt 20:26), and "All who exalt themselves will be humbled. . . ." (Matt 23:12). Jesus himself washed the feet of his disciples, a service which even slaves at that time could not be compelled to do. My words paraphrase the word "humility" *(demut)* which in German means "the courage to serve." Likewise, going higher and higher up the ladder for the sake of prestige, will do good for the marriage only if it is done in an attitude of humility, which avoids putting unreasonable demands on the other party.

So we wish for you that with this ladder in your marriage you may once again get hold of the bird of paradise, even if you are not able to hold it fast. Now I am happy to bind your hands with this stole which is decorated with the emblem of Christ. If you allow him to be in your midst, no one will be able to tear you down.

Scripture Index

	Homily Number	*Page Number*
Gen 2:18-25	4	11
Gen 9:12-17	14	39
Gen 12:1-17	24	69
Ps 23	38	111
Eccl 4:9-12	20, 28, 29, 38, 40	56, 81, 84, 111, 117
Song Solomon 8:6-7	4, 6, 22, 30, 37	11, 17, 63, 87, 108
Matt 5:14-16	6, 10, 23, 37	17, 28, 66, 108
Matt 5:23-26	10, 18, 27, 37	28, 51, 79, 108
Matt 5:23-26	16	46
Matt 6:25-33	21	59
Matt 7:12	21	59
Matt 7:24-27	5, 15, 17	14, 43, 51
Matt 13:45	29	84
Matt 14:22-23	1	1
Matt 17:1-9	28, 30	81, 87
Matt 18:21f.	14, 16, 39	39, 46, 114
Matt 19:3-6	4, 29	11, 84
Matt 20:25-28	40	117
Matt 22:35-40	12, 31	32, 90
Matt 25:1-13	27	79
Mark 10:6-9	19	54
Luke 15:11-24	4	11
Luke 24:13-35	24, 38	69, 111
John 2:1-11	11	30
John 3:16-18	2	5
John 14:1-6	38	111
John 15:1-5	2, 8, 12, 18, 22, 25, 31, 36, 38, 40	5, 23, 32, 51, 63, 72, 90, 105, 111, 117
John 15:1-5, 9-12	7, 34, 36	20, 99, 105

	Homily Number	*Page Number*
John 15:9-12	1, 3, 4, 9, 12, 17, 21, 26, 28, 30, 33, 34, 35, 36	1, 8, 11, 25, 32, 49, 59, 76, 81, 87, 95, 99, 102, 105
John 15:12, 13, 17	20	56
Rom 12:9-18	7, 25	20, 72
Rom 13:8-10	9, 22, 32	25, 63, 93
1 Cor 1:18-31	2	5
1 Cor 13:4-8a	1, 8, 20, 26, 28, 30, 32, 39	1, 23, 56, 76, 81, 87, 93, 114
1 Cor 13:4-8a, 13	3, 17, 18, 19, 35, 39	8, 49, 51, 54, 102, 114
Eph 4:29-32	14	39
Eph 4:29-32; 5:1f.	5, 9, 15, 16	14, 25, 43, 46
Phil 4:4-9	21, 27	59, 79
Col 3:12-15	5, 7, 8, 9, 14, 15, 16, 18, 23, 25, 27, 33, 40	14, 20, 23, 25, 39, 43, 46, 51, 66, 72, 79, 95, 117
Col 3:12-14 (-17)	13	35
Col 4:9-12	20, 21, 28, 29, 38, 40	56, 59, 81, 84, 111, 117
1 Thess 5:15-18	9, 23, 25, 26	25, 66, 72, 76
1 Pet 2:5-10	8	23
1 Pet 3:8-15a	7, 16, 23, 26	20, 46, 66, 76
1 John 2:7-11	10	28
1 John 4:7-12:	2	5
1 John 4:16b-19	18, 34, 36	51, 99, 105
1 John 4:16b-21	12, 31	32, 90